The Secular as Methodology

The Secular as Methodology

A Christian View of the Benefits and Dangers of Secularization

Robert L. Montgomery

WIPF & STOCK · Eugene, Oregon

THE SECULAR AS METHODOLOGY
A Christian View of the Benefits and Dangers of Secularization

Copyright © 2018 Robert L. Montgomery. All rights reserved. Except for brief quotations in critical publications or reviews, no part of this book may be reproduced in any manner without prior written permission from the publisher. Write: Permissions, Wipf and Stock Publishers, 199 W. 8th Ave., Suite 3, Eugene, OR 97401.

Wipf & Stock
An Imprint of Wipf and Stock Publishers
199 W. 8th Ave., Suite 3
Eugene, OR 97401

www.wipfandstock.com

PAPERBACK ISBN: 978-1-5326-5764-1
HARDCOVER ISBN: 978-1-5326-5765-8
EBOOK ISBN: 978-1-5326-5766-5

Manufactured in the U.S.A.

Dedicated to my teachers and colleagues who helped
me wrestle with the secular as methodology

Contents

Preface | ix
Introduction | xix

Chapter 1: My Intellectual Exploration and Spiritual Journey | 1
Chapter 2: The Emergence of the Secular | 11
Chapter 3: Why the Secular Revolution | 25
Chapter 4: Secular Methodology in Science | 37
Chapter 5: Secular Methodology in Government | 51
Chapter 6: Secular Methodology in Education | 60
Chapter 7: Secular Methodology in the Family | 78
Chapter 8: Secular Methodology in Everyday Life | 87
Chapter 9: Secular Methodology in Theology | 93
Chapter 10: Future of the Secular | 102

Appendix: Secular Methodology in Missiology | 111
Bibliography | 115
Index | 119

Preface

THROUGH MUCH OF MY life because of my faith as a Christian, there was no such thing as secular to me. I was barely familiar with the word. There was a world out there beyond my family and the church, but I believed God was everywhere and working in and through all things. That does not mean I understood what God was doing, but I assumed God's overall control and God's presence and work throughout the world in all things. I learned from my parents that though there was evil in the world (and I saw it and sometimes felt it in myself), the world was not all bad and in fact, much good could be learned and enjoyed in the world because God created a good world. The bad was basically self-destructive and the good self-rewarding. The line between the church and the world was not clear cut but somewhat fuzzy because God was in both the church and the world. There was good and bad in both, but the church was God's chosen instrument for spreading the gospel of Jesus Christ. In this respect, I was raised a mainline Christian who felt free to enjoy much that was in the world, but above all to enjoy the Christian life and community as the place of God's special activity. As I learned in the Westminster Shorter Catechism, "Man's chief end is to glorify God and to enjoy him forever."[1] I liked that.

I became aware early on in the mission field in China where my parents lived and worked, that there were Christians who saw much evil in the world and wanted to draw a very clear line between themselves and the world, including non-Christians and even Christians who were considered unorthodox. Later in life I came to see they were like the people Paul mentioned as not wanting to eat food that had been offered to idols (Rom 14:13–23; 1 Cor 8). They were to be respected and not unnecessarily upset in their beliefs, but I did not need to follow their strict

---

1. "Shorter Catechism, Question 1," *Westminster Confession of Faith*, 7.001, 205.

ways while respecting, listening to, and learning from them. I have come to see many conservative Christians, their churches, and their schools, somewhat in that light.

Because of the faith of my parents and our Christian community, I lived in effect under a religious canopy much like most premodern people who believed they were surrounded by superhuman powers, although their superhuman powers were quite different from ours.[2] A religious canopy still exists for many people in the world. It still exists for me, although I recognize that this canopy or umbrella not only exists over me as an individual, but it also existed over my parents and exists over the larger community of faith to which we belonged and to which I still belong. But for me, it was not just a matter of assenting to statements of faith or accepting a religious tradition as a matter of course, which apparently a religious canopy has often meant to many people past and present. It was a matter of a reality to which I belonged and to which I eventually committed myself to serve as an ordained pastor.

I believe the faith canopy (distinguished from a more general religious canopy) is much stronger than many secularists realize, but not the older religious canopy. And the faith canopy is not just private, as some scholars of religion in the modern era like to assert, but includes communities of faith and love. However, I now realize that for many people a secular canopy exists over society as a whole and consequently some people decide to be secular like their imagined canopy, but others, who fear the secular canopy, decide to withdraw from what they regard as a secularized society. Still others, like me, decide to participate in a society that is based on God's good creation, but accept a faith canopy for themselves as individuals and their faith community as they accept and commit to the overall reality of God and the specific reality of God's revelation in Jesus Christ. That revelation seen in the Bible is the key to life for me in this world and the next. The general religious canopy used to require only an agreement or assent to God's or other superhuman realities, but now more than ever a conscious decision needs to be made to believe in it and commit to God. This has been called "the faith option" and its clarification, paradoxically, is probably the most important long-range result of the various secularizing influences, as we shall see.[3] In reality, the believer finds that this option is not so much

---

2. I am adopting Christian Smith's terminology of "superhuman" rather than "supernatural." See his definition of religion in my chapter 2 and in Smith, *Religion*, 22.

3. I get this concept from the book by Hans Joas, *The Faith Option*, but also have

our choice as an acceptance of God's choice of us. On the one hand, the Protestant Reformation made secularization possible by questioning the established religious authority, but surprisingly and paradoxically, now secularization is helping to clarify faith. Is this not God's working in history so that people will have to decide to come out from hiding as they realize God has come in Christ "walking on earth" asking "Where are you?," (Gen 3:8, 9) and also specifically, "Who do you say that I am" (Mark 8:29)? The options then and now are to hide or not answer, or to say "here I am" and "help me follow where you lead." That is my belief. In other words, strange as it may seem, I believe God has brought us to this point where the secular can even become an instrument for good and bring clarification of the faith option to choose God or not, or to recognize God's choice of us or not.

From what I have just said, you can see that for me (to make a definition) the secular is primarily a mental construct, without ontological reality apart from being human thought. There are two forms of this secular mental construct. In the first one, any idea of God is considered to be based in unreality or at least irrelevant to life. The second secular mental construct is more complex because it recognizes the reality and activity of God in the world and God's personal presence (obviously a faith perspective), but sets aside or brackets any ideas of God's causation of anything in order to improve or correct ideas about the world and God's actions in the world. I am emphasizing that the believer never sets aside her or his faith in God's presence and purpose. Rather, in the second form of mental construct, while believers maintain their own religious beliefs they recognize that their own ideas of God, of human life, and the world are partial and flawed and always need improvement. This distinguishes faith and ideas coming from faith. The Christian's ideas of God and of creation, including human beings, come primarily from interpretations of the Bible, but these ideas necessarily come with much use of secular methodologies, be they scientific or simple observation. This second secular mental construct is based on the belief that God is distinct from creation but not separate from it. Instead, God works in all of creation to uphold every part of it and display God's glory. (Believing this "panentheism" may make some theologians, such as Jonathan Edwards, even sound like pantheists when they are not.)

---

been influenced by Joas' very balanced view of the continuing presence and influence of religion along with secularizing influences. I will be drawing on Charles Taylor later, but David Brooks in the *New York Times* points to Taylor emphasizing that in the secular age "Religious faith or non-faith becomes more a matter of personal choice as part of a quest for personal development" (lines 62–65).

In addition to nature, God is also, or even more, active in human history to work out God's will. On the one hand, the activity of God in nature and history, including in the Bible itself, can only be perceived by faith and cannot be demonstrated or proven by human investigation. On the other hand, the second mental construct recognizes that nature and history operate in a way that are discoverable and since God made us responsible for the advancement of knowledge, the care of the world, and for the care of humankind under God, we need to seek to understand nature and history by utilizing secular methodologies, which are more systematic and reliable than simple observation. In other words, incorporated in the faith perspective are ideas about creation (both nature and history) that we need to gain by secular methodologies in order to make the best use of the knowledge we gain from them. Some might make the secular out to be equivalent to nature (creation), but the secular does not have ontological reality apart from existence as human thoughts, whereas nature as creation has ontological reality so that nature and human life as part of nature can be studied apart from God. God cannot be taken out of anything by our secular mental constructs, but since all we can think and express about God are our ideas (and we relate to God by faith, not our ideas), those ideas are what we leave out when carrying out a secular methodology of study or activity. We do it for a purpose, namely to improve or correct our ideas and activities in the world and the world itself, which is under God's judgment working in all things. As our ideas are improved or corrected, our faith relationship to God can also be clarified and strengthened. I might add, we want to avoid "taking God's name in vain" (the third commandment) by attributing facts or events to God incorrectly and secular methodology helps us to avoid taking God's name in vain, even when we say "the Bible says." Those who do not believe in God are free to think about and study God's creation or simply act in it as though God did not exist. They may thus gain some understanding of it and may have a good or bad effect upon it as a result. How the understanding and activity aided by secular methodology will be used and what kind of effect the activity will have remains an open question. Faith certainly comes into play in how we use knowledge gained by secular methodologies.

Let us remember that although we Christians believe God is real, God is still an imperfect mental construct for us because we have partial and imperfect ideas of God and God's creation (our theology.) However, we believe God is helping us to construct our ideas of God through "the means of grace," especially the Bible, the sacraments, prayer, and the community of faith (based on Acts 2:42), all of which are under the Holy Spirit. But God is always beyond our ideas, yet also supportive of our ideas that are true. Mainly, faith is not an idea, but a relationship which may be attended by real but imperfect feelings or sensibilities. True faith or the living relationship with God is real because it is a gift of God, but whatever we think or say about our faith becomes our theology and is inevitably partial. Christians seek also to have the inner feelings and sensibilities that often go with faith, including when planning or doing a secular activity. Feelings of joy or peace often follow acts of faith for which we are grateful, but a Christian acts in faith, not simply to create good feelings. Craig Barnes clarified the priority of faith over feelings of certainty, which is often forgotten by Christians.[4] Thus a scientist, a politician, or anyone else in everyday life can certainly think or work with faith which may be accompanied by a varying sense of God's presence and guidance and by varying feelings.

Basically, Christians, when using a secular methodology in study or activity, do not attribute causation to God. That is a separate theological activity. They let their ideas and actions based on secular methodology stand on their own under God's and human judgment in a world that stands on its own, but that God has nevertheless given over to humankind to use in service to God. Of the two judgments, of course God's takes priority, and we believe God's is made through the grace in Jesus Christ who died for us and has forgiven us. In short, a secular methodology not only means thinking with a certain mental construction (in which causation is not attributed to God), but also acting in the physical or material world in certain ways that are effective in and of themselves. These may be done with or without faith. In other words, nature and human life have to be respected and dealt with on their own terms. In secular methodology in everyday life, for example, hard work and honesty can be fruitful. I hasten to add to what I have said above that the person of faith can and should use a secular methodology while remaining conscious of God, and offer up the effort and results to God. In this way, ideas of God, the self, and the world can be useful for human life, as well as for the kingdom of God.

Ideas are powerful and ideas about God, right or wrong, good or bad, can have an effect on our lives, in society, and in history. These ideas are certainly useful to study with a secular methodology, even though as Christians we may and should also subject them to theological judgment based

---

4. Barnes, "Uncertain and faithful," 35.

on God's revelation in the Bible, but primarily in Jesus Christ. Ideas about God are central in Christian theology, but they are based on what is believed in and, very importantly, they should be gained from the interpreted self-revelation of God in the Bible that has a long history in Christian tradition. (Others may look to other revelations, but I am writing as a Christian.) In other words, it is through that revelation in Jesus Christ and the Bible, together with the Spirit that inspired them, that our ideas about God are constructed, but they should be gained in the Christian tradition and not simply gained and held privately. I believe theological seminaries are part of God's plan as a means of setting people apart for the study of God's word (Acts 6:1, 2). In secular studies of religion, almost all religions have religious specialists. Secularists in society called intellectuals can also form their own communities based on common ideas and shared tasks, but they are far from stable. Nevertheless, Christians may gain knowledge from secular scholars and even form communities or schools of thought with them. I think it is important to note that Christianity, from its earliest days, was organized, with every member honored for having special gifts and tasks.

It is important that theology incorporate the secular study of religion, but the secular study of religion cannot incorporate theology except to view it as a human expression and activity. Theology needs to consider itself as fallible human thinking too, even as it seeks to interpret God's revelation, but theology also seeks to encompass all of reality, not just the limited reality viewed by the secular approach of science or any other secular approach. In other words, secular methodology cannot theorize about God (only ideas about God and activities based on those ideas) or attribute causes to God (as theology does), but sees theology or belief in God's activity and activity on behalf of God only as a type of human thought and activity. Thus, theology has its own methodology, which is primarily to interpret Jesus Christ and the Bible as God's self-revelation in an organized fashion. Included in theology is knowledge that has been gained from the humanities and the natural and social sciences, and that contributes to a perspective toward total reality, especially human strengths and failings.

As a construction of the mind and also simply human activity, the secular can be used as a label for activities, goals, ethics, organizations, large institutions, and modes of thought and activity which are not specifically termed as religious. This is because the modern world, unlike the ancient or traditional world distinguishes between religion and the secular.

Yet secular thoughts and activities may be used for religious or sacred purposes, especially when humans benefit. The Christian is challenged to offer those thoughts and activities (and the humans benefited) up to God. But the secular approach to all things, as we shall see, has become quite powerful so that it is possible to speak of the secular mind in which the secular perspective (a world without God) is dominant.[5] The secular then becomes a kind of sensibility. Like all beliefs, the mental construction and approach to life that many modern people have is that there is no God or if there is, God is irrelevant. However, when they say they do not believe in God, it is their idea of God, not God's actual self that they do not believe in. The sad fact is that the idea of God that they do not believe in may have come from what they observed in, or learned from, Christians. For example, they may not like the idea of a primarily judgmental God, particularly as represented by some Christians. The approach to life with the concept and label of the secular is a powerful legacy of secularizing influences.[6] However, as noted above, I do not believe that in secular thought and activities we cannot be conscious of God. Far from it. It only means we bracket our ideas of causation by God in whom we believe (we keep a sense of God's presence) in order to humbly learn more about God's actions and free our ideas from our human distorted thinking. Thus, surprisingly, using the secular as a methodology is an act of humility for Christians. As noted, one of the main effects of secularizing the influences of our time is simply to distinguish the religious from the secular, which former societies did not do (except the church itself when the secular simply meant the world at large where parish priests worked). You can probably tell that like many mainline Christians I do not like constantly referring to God or the Lord. In other words, it is best to let our "yes" be "yes" and our "no" be "no" rather than show our piety by mentioning God or the Lord, "the good Lord" being a favorite somewhat patronizing reference to the Lord (Matt 5:33–37).

Thus, from my faith perspective the secular does not exist ontologically, but is only in the mind. I realize that this is exactly the opposite from the view of a secularist or a nonbeliever. In their nonfaith view, nature is the only reality and God does not exist ontologically, but is only a mental construct. To them, the secular methodology deals with the only reality and there is no reality beyond it. In other words, the followers of

---

5. Coles, *Secular Mind*.

6. I accept Smith's view that "secularization" is best understood as a number of various processes (*Religion*, 243–55).

secularism (note the "ism") are following an ideology in which God either does not exist or is irrelevant to life. Yet I hasten to add that some secularists may advocate and act with a higher morality and with truer ideas of the world than many religious people who nevertheless profess to be Christians. Thinking and acting morally and immorally are human characteristics. That is why it is so important to learn what can be learned from secularists, as well as followers of other religions. Humility about our own ideas requires it. Theologically, the good ideas of secularists or of other religions are the result of common grace, which is extended to all humanity and certainly is seen in many religions. Thus, having a moral sensibility is simply a human trait, part of the image of God. The secular may be applied to an era or a culture, such as our present one with its secular canopy and labels in the minds of many. But our era may not be as secular as some people think with all of the individual and community faith canopies such as I and others share and enjoy. A secular methodology, diligently applied, is the worst enemy of false ideas, but of course secular methodologies are never perfectly applied.

In this book I want to show that the secular is not necessarily opposed to an active faith, but can be very useful as a methodology in which our ideas of God as a cause in our lives, in nature, and in the world are bracketed for a special purpose—to give protection from, and correction to, false ideas and practices, some of which, perhaps too many, are given a religious, and unfortunately a Christian, label. Both true and false religious ideas about God and activities for God can be important causal factors in the world and so if we believe in the need for continuing clarification and reforming of faith and faith communities, then secular methodologies are necessary and useful instruments for clarifying true ideas. I believe the basic reason for the bracketing of the attribution of causes to God is based on an important theological doctrine: total depravity, which means that all ("total") human thinking, including theological thinking, is tainted by sin and therefore fallible. I believe in the revelation of God in the Bible and especially in Jesus Christ, which inevitably I and others must interpret. Our interpretations will be incomplete and sometimes rather seriously mistaken, especially as we Christians live out our interpretation. Since we are part of a created universe, secular methodology based on taking the world seriously for what it is as God's good creation thus can be a useful corrective to human thinking, including thinking about God that has been gained from faulty or incomplete interpretations of Jesus Christ and the Bible.

PREFACE

If we are Christians, we believe and hope that the construction of God in our minds and the activities of our bodies come from the work of God's Spirit through the revelation of God in the Bible and especially in Jesus Christ, but we need to be humble about that construction and our activities, which are undoubtedly influenced by our sin and are very partial. The Christian community and our families are the major means of creating all that we know about God and certainly influence how we act. But now in our secular age, it is increasingly important to know our knowledge of God and all that is related to God will always be partial and marred by sin. Paul knew this, but Christians tend to forget that "for now we see in a mirror, dimly ... now I know only in part" (1 Cor 13:12). We will only know God and the whole truth that is embodied in Jesus Christ in the next life, but now our thoughts about God and our activities for God are very incomplete. This is why Paul emphasized love as the most important aspect of the life and work of the Christian: "Knowledge puffs up, but love builds up" (1 Cor 8:1). This lets us know that faith is primarily a relationship of trust and love that is expressed in action, and not simply an idea or way of thinking. It is not fully expressible or livable. Since all of our knowledge of God, namely religious knowledge, is partial and marred by sin, it means that it is very useful to lay this knowledge aside or bracket it at times in order to correct and improve it. Secular methodologies aid in doing this. Unfortunately, religious people, perhaps especially we Christians who should know better, have advanced many wrong ideas and worse, perpetrated many evils in the world. It has become especially clear that Christians and whole Christian communities may espouse and support wrong and even evil causes.

I hope to show that the most useful way to regard the secular is as a methodology or rather a set of methodologies, which can help to prevent the misuse of religion (ideas and activities related to God). At the same time, secular methodologies may correct and improve human thinking about the world and human activity in controlling governments, institutions, and people's lives in the wrong way. The secular canopy over modern society is not as disturbing to me as it is for many Christians (and Muslims) because I have come to see the secular as providing very useful methodologies, which actually give protection from, and correction to, human thought and action, especially religious thought and action. This means that the secular, surprisingly and paradoxically, can be used to perform sacred purposes. I believe the fear of secular humanism is misplaced because secular humanism can be mixed with Christian humanism so that both Christians and secularists can contribute to, and participate in, many activities that benefit humanity. At the same time, I recognize, as already noted, that the secular can be very dangerous as it becomes an idol, like nature, for some people. As with all God's gifts it can be misused. The worship of the secular is actually self-worship.

I decided to write this book partly because of the bad reputation of the secular among many Christians, but especially to encourage the use of the secular to clarify the gospel of Jesus Christ and the faith option to choose God, or rather accept God's choice of us, that is challenging the modern person. I believe it takes both faith and also secular skill in using the secular to expose and clarify the forces that affect us because many of them are outside of our consciousness. If used well, secular methodologies can be one of the major tools to enable the church to experience corrections and be a better representative of the gospel of Jesus Christ. Secular methodologies can even be a means of bringing people of different faiths and viewpoints together where they can listen to, and learn from, each other.

Introduction

IN THIS BOOK I consider how people of faith and anyone else can understand the secular in modern life and use a variety of secular methods in useful ways. My approach is rather personal as I describe what the secular has meant to me as a concept and as a set of methodologies for life. My major point is that the secular is anything and everything considered apart from our ideas of God as a causal factor. But it can be seen and used as a methodology to protect us from wrong and harmful ideas and activities, especially religious ones, and especially as a useful tool to advance knowledge and lead a healthy personal and civic life. Notice that God in reality is not bracketed (we cannot take God out of anything), but it is our ideas or interpretations (not sensibility) of God that are bracketed, though temporarily. In any case, those of a secular mindset or nonbelievers do not consider the reality of God, but as Christians we offer up what we do and learn with a secular methodology in service to God.

There are many positive benefits from the right use of secular methodologies that improve human life. Consider modern medicine, as well as many modern improvements in our standard of living that we often take for granted unless we have lived without them. Even or maybe especially well-done ordinary tasks can improve life. As Christians we believe the Bible, our faith, and the church have divine origins, but we cannot escape the fact that they are also human activities and products and can be looked at that way even though we believe God works through them. Seen this way, secular methodology paradoxically can be a means of deepening faith. Secular methodology is particularly made sacred as it is offered up to God in service, but of course secular methodology may be used with no thought of service to God and may be used against the will of God. There is no way to avoid taking account of secular methodologies because we are surrounded by them, and as humans we are subject to examination by them. A modern education requires that we learn some of them.

The preface already expresses some of my basic ideas about secular methodology, but in chapter 1, I will try to explain how I got to my present views about the secular and secular methodology. It is an intellectual and spiritual pilgrimage and a struggle that is still going on. In chapters 2 and 3, I briefly tell the complex history of the emergence of the secular. Some might say this emergence was an escape from the domination of religion, or at least the domination of the institutional aspect of religion. The secular emerged to be in contrast to religion, both being mental constructions and activities that have very real consequences. They both demonstrate the power of the mind and ideologies. I believe secularization draws on realities built in to creation and human nature, but also has a great deal to with resistance to the domination of religion. Some do not like their faith characterized as a religion, but I believe humility requires recognizing Christianity as a human institution or rather group of institutions and practices and therefore a religion. The existence of the human side of Christianity is a major reason why the secular provides useful tools or methodologies, not for understanding God directly, but nevertheless for learning much about what God is doing in the world and in the church through human beings, and points toward what we ought to be doing in the church and the world.

In chapters 4 through 9, I discuss what I believe are six major positive uses of the secular as a methodology, namely as a methodology in science, government, education, the family, everyday life, and finally theology itself. There are certainly other aspects of life that could be considered. My discussions in these chapters will be mainly in terms of my own struggles with secular methodologies. There are many elaborations of the areas discussed where the secular provides useful methodologies, most of which may be shared both by people of faith and those who are without faith. This may be one of the major advantages of recognizing and using secular methodologies—they allow people to work together regardless of what their faith position may or many not be. On the one hand, these methodologies protect believers and nonbelievers from the misuse and misunderstandings of religion by religious and other people. At the same time, believers and nonbelievers are also protected from the misunderstandings and misuses of the secular by the same methodologies. The secular used as a methodology limits and controls secular opinions of which secularism, the ideology, is

INTRODUCTION

one. In short, I believe secular methodologies help to protect both religion and the secular from misuse by the other.

The future of the secular and its methodologies is not fully clear in a world where there have been different understandings and reactions to the process of secularization. In chapter 10, I discuss what I believe may be the future of the secular in the United States and in global society, as unclear as this may be. Whatever the case, the secular may be perceived as both a friend and a foe, even a powerful foe, but it also has feet of clay, as we have seen with those who thought religion was passing away. I believe recognizing and using the secular as a source for methodologies is the best way of perceiving it as a friend. This means also understanding the limitations of the secular as a methodology.

I am writing this brief book from a Christian faith perspective, albeit one that has been chastened and, I hope, improved by my encounter with the secular. Instead of drawing me away from my faith, my experience in thinking about and dealing with the secular has drawn me ever deeper into the life of faith. I understand that we are increasingly living in a world of diverse religions and nonreligion, and that it is highly important that we listen to each other. Even though the gospel has been presented in a way that makes it appear to exclude entirely the messages of other religions, I believe we can learn much from each other. The exclusion is not as clear as some would make it out to be. Furthermore, Jesus did not impose his gospel, but issued an open invitation for people to come to him (Matt 11:28–30) and very importantly, to follow him, which is different from following a set of rules. Christians have used coercion, but Jesus never did. And he never claimed any territory for God other than the whole world, as some Christians and Jews have claimed territory. His purpose was to be a means of drawing all people to God through himself (John 12:32). His constant use of "follow me" shows his recognition that he was a path or way to God in himself. Different societies have had the concept of a universal Way, for example *logos* to the Greeks and *dao* to the Chinese. This should give confidence to Christians as they communicate with the peoples of world how Jesus fulfills a universal movement in creation. Unfortunately, the sense of imposition of Christianity in societies and families has been a major basis for opposition to, and rejection of, Christianity, and unfortunately the gospel with it. I believe the end work of God in secular history will be to lead humanity toward a sense of freedom in choosing to live in fellowship with the God who created and loves all people and who ultimately chooses us. I

INTRODUCTION

call this the completion of the circle of love or the way that began with God, extends through history, and returns to the Creator.

I want to acknowledge the able help of Brian Palmer in copy editing and Calvin Jaffarian in type setting the text in preparation for publication. Previously, many people contributed to my thoughts on the subject of the secular. I must mention Charles Robinson, a professor of chemistry for many years at Memphis State University, who is now in retirement but is active in the arts—writing, music, and theater. His ancestor, John Robinson, spoke to the departing Pilgrims, who were part of his congregation in Leiden, Netherlands, saying that "he was very confident the Lord had more truth and light yet to break forth out of his holy Word."[7] This has been an important truth to me as I see God using the secular to do just that. Charles read the complete early draft and had numerous helpful comments. Bruce Greenawalt, a longtime teacher of history, and Fitzhugh Legerton, having served on college boards, were especially helpful on the difficult subject of the secular in Christian education. William Hoyt, a professor of religion, was very helpful in regard to John Calvin's view of truth beyond the Bible and Christian humanism. W. Michael Smith, a former missionary to Ethiopia and Indonesia who worked many years with Bread for the World, was very helpful in expressing to me the dynamic reality of the universal Way. William (Bill) Janes contributed useful thoughts to me on the doctrine of parentheism. Eugene I. (Gene) Earnhardt and the Saturday norming discussion group contributed many ideas to me. In addition to Gene, Bruce (Greenawalt) and me, this group consisted mainly of Gerald L. (Jerry) Argall, Robert (Bob) Bennett, George Duncan, James F. (Jim) Earnhardt, Hugh Richard (Dick) Graham, Robert E. (Bob) Riddle, Robert M. Smith, and William (Bill) Spellman. Finally, I want to thank Kao Chun-Ming, former General Secretary of the Presbyterian Church in Taiwan, and James A. Cogswell, both of whom were above me in the church—they encouraged me in my plans for further study to clarify the causes for the aboriginal Christian movement that led eventually to my encounter with the secular as methodology. Of course, I must take responsibility for my views on all points expressed in this book.

---

7. Burgess, *John Robinson*, 240.

CHAPTER 1

My Intellectual Exploration and Spiritual Journey

IN ORDER TO CLARIFY how I came to hold the views expressed in this book, I need to tell you about my intellectual exploration up to this point, along with my spiritual journey, which is still evolving. It was not until I went back to graduate school at Emory University at age thirty-nine to take up the social scientific study of religion that I encountered what seemed to be an artificially created secular realm of the mind and also of activity. I was looking for some reasons for the remarkable Christian movement I had witnessed in Taiwan.[1] I quickly learned that important truths could be learned about human behavior by putting aside my previous theological approach. I had been a history major in college (Rhodes College), followed by theological training in two seminaries (Columbia and Princeton Theological Seminaries). At Emory, I soon learned that the social sciences, like the natural sciences, are intentionally scientific in approach, which clearly employs a secular methodology. Since the social sciences are considered soft sciences, and maybe not really scientific in approach, I found that my teachers seemed to bend over backwards to teach scientific methodology. We spent time studying scientific research methods, including statistical methods. At any rate, in terms of being secular, any attribution of cause to God for anything in human life, even or especially in religious life, was ruled out in social scientific studies of religion.

As a result of my previous studies in theological seminaries, I tended to look at everything theologically and particularly through the perspective of the Bible. As Calvin pointed out, the Scriptures are like "spectacles"

---

1. My major conclusions were published after a period of exploration in 2012: Montgomery, *Why Religions Spread*.

for viewing God and everything else.[2] I should also say that Calvin was a Christian humanist who saw truth, wisdom, and morality in human beings apart from the church. He was part of the humanistic movement in Europe. He wrote a commentary on Seneca's *De Clementia* and had great respect for Cicero's thoughts. Calvin, in fact, goes to great lengths to emphasize that the "light of truth" is "admirably displayed" in the works of "heathen writers" and that "If we believe the Spirit of God is the only fountain of truth, we shall neither reject nor despise the truth itself, wherever it should appear . . ."[3] The term "science" was not yet in common use and meant primarily systematic study. Theology was the queen of sciences. Those we now know as scientists were called philosophers. Calvin said, "Shall we say that the philosophers were blind in their exquisite contemplation and in their scientific description of nature?"[4] Because of Calvin's humanism, I like to be careful in criticizing humanism. I recognize that humanism can become an idol, but so can the church or Christian fellowship groups, and also, sadly, the Bible, as in bibliolatry or biblicism.[5] Calvin's humanistic side, as well as that of Reformed theology and its openness to secular knowledge, probably prepared me to seek understanding in the social sciences after I encountered the overwhelming experience of being with aboriginal Christians who responded so enthusiastically to the gospel of Jesus Christ. I did not feel that my college and seminary studies had prepared me adequately to understand what happened.

In graduate school and subsequently, the study of religion and everything else from a secular perspective was a strong reminder to me of what I was told had taken place in the modern world—the process of secularization. However, I discovered there was an enormous debate among social scientists about the meaning of secularization and its related terms, such as secularism and secularity. I do not plan to enter this debate here, but to focus on the secular as an aspect of thought and life that emerged in the modern world to be in contrast to religious thought, activity, and organizations. Of course both realms—religious and secular—have always been present, but only in the modern world have they become so clearly

---

2. Calvin, *Institutes of the Christian Religion*, 1:73, 74.

3. Interestingly, the term "heathen writers" is used in the 1818 translation of the Institutes, but the modern translation by John T. McNeill uses the term "secular writers," apparently as a softer term than "heathen." However, "secular" with the modern meaning was not used by Calvin.

4. Calvin, Institutes, 2:216–17.

5. Smith, *Bible Made Impossible*.

distinguished in human thought. I will discuss this development in the following two chapters.

Many sociologists considered only the effect of society on religion and assumed that religion would eventually succumb to the secular when people realized religion's irrationality. One professor told me religion was best studied primarily as a dependent variable. The professor meant that religion was best understood as an entity affected by its social context or external conditions and not as also affecting its social context or external conditions. In addition to basic scientific methodology, I now think all theologians should study the sociology of knowledge, a subject which Karl Marx pioneered, but ultimately failed in his attempt to present a comprehensive view of the mutual interaction between religion and society. Many students are shocked to learn how much they have been affected by their social and material context and subsequently react by rejecting their background entirely. This extreme reaction is certainly not necessary; in fact one need only critically recognize the limitations of their background and the harm sometimes done in it to themselves and others. I could accept the value of emphasizing the influence of social and material contexts for understanding some aspects of religions, but I was also very conscious of how people of faith have affected the world for both good and bad, namely representing religion as an independent variable. Many social scientists seem to have forgotten that the founders of the discipline, Emile Durkheim (1858–1918) and Max Weber (1884–1920), recognized the real effects of religious beliefs on individuals and on social and economic life.[6] Relatively late in my studies after graduate school, I found a well-known sociologist of religion, Rodney Stark, who specifically considered how monotheistic religions impacted human history, including through missions, my special area of interest.[7] Because I believed that God was active in the world and affecting both individuals and the historical process, I felt the need to reconcile my social scientific studies with my theological thought and also my calling to be a minister of the gospel. I was concerned that some among my own family and friends would think I was leaving my calling as a minister of the gospel of Jesus Christ.

Early in my studies of the social sciences I was greatly impressed by Robert Merton's, as a sociologist of science, description of "the ethos of

---

6. Durkheim, *Elementary Forms*, 479; Weber, *Protestant Ethic and the Spirit*.

7. Stark, *Rise of Christianity*. Stark also makes clear in *One True God* that the content of religions can have powerful effects in human history.

science."[8] I believe his ethos of science shows the power that a secular approach to knowledge can have, but also the degree to which it is guided by often unrecognized norms. Taken together, how different it was from the ethos of theological inquiry in which I had been trained! And yet there was some overlap. Very briefly, Merton identified the norms which characterized the ethos of science as *universalism, communism, disinterestedness,* and *organized skepticism. Universalism* requires that truth-claims, whatever their source, are to be subjected to preestablished impersonal criteria. *Communism* definitely has no reference to the political ideology, but to the norm that science is part of the public domain and findings must be widely communicated. *Universal sharing* (my term) might be less misleading in light of the history of communism as a destructive force. In terms of sharing work and findings, I noticed that there was a strong sociology of religion community of scholars existing within sociology, which exists within the larger community of the social sciences. There are three North American sociology of religion associations with overlapping memberships that meet regularly, but I was always disappointed to see many seminaries poorly represented at their meetings. I have never understood how seminaries could ignore the scholars who make it their specialty to study the field of theologians. I even encountered among scholars (including many friends) a tendency to look down on the social sciences, particularly sociology of religion. This probably strengthens the sense of community among sociology of religion scholars. At any rate scientists are expected to share their findings and theorizing as widely as possible. *Disinterestedness* requires that personal motives should be separated from questions regarding the truth of findings. *Organized skepticism* requires that a critical stance be taken toward every aspect of nature and society. Later, Merton added the norms of *originality* and *humility*.[9] *Originality* means that scientists should be constantly seeking new knowledge, and *humility* means not a personal characteristic of scientists, but the need for scientists to recognize that their work will be largely replaced in the future as new knowledge is added. Perhaps you can see why I was impressed by such an ethos, especially since some theologians feel free to assert their beliefs with great confidence, not recognizing them as their interpretations of the Bible, not the Bible itself in its original meaning or total emphasis! The confident assertion of one

---

8. Merton. "Normative Structure of Science," 267–78.
9. Ibid., 286–324, 384–412.

opinion seems to almost be a requirement for those in the arts and to some extent in the humanities generally, including theology!

Another early discovery in reading about the social sciences was Herbert Spencer's emphasis on the universality of bias in his book, *The Study of Sociology*.[10] He described educational bias, the bias of patriotism, class bias, political bias, and theological bias (including anti-theological bias). I had already learned that in the social sciences bias was a technical term meaning a personal and inevitably partial perspective, which the scientific method seeks to control, not simply personal prejudice. The control of bias is one of the main tasks of the scientific method. Its universality reminded me of the Christian concept of sin, under which Spencer had been raised as a Dissenter in England, though he eventually became an agnostic. I wrote my first article after graduate school on Spencer's concept of bias.[11]

Interestingly, although scientific studies should follow a method that accords with the norms identified by Merton, the one part of a scientific study involving an unscientific choice is the choice of a topic to study. To me this blows a large hole in what some might boast to be their scientific approach. The fact is that people live by their normative views, which are often simply opinions that are highly biased in both the technical and nontechnical sense. My personal normative views came into play from the start because I chose my study topic—the spread of religions—on the basis of my personal faith and interest. Interestingly, Merton, a specialist in the sociology of science, wrote his first major study on the influence of Puritans, who came from a Christian context, on early science in England.[12] I must add that the sociologist Rodney Stark goes farther back to the Middle Ages to argue that the scientific movement would not have taken place without the belief of the "natural philosophers" in the rationality of God and God's creation, enabling humans to uncover patterns and exceptions to patterns within nature and develop great benefits to human life.[13]

Merton's views on the ethos of science were very important to me because of the strong implication that science ultimately rests on the ethos of a free society where studies may be critical of those with social, economic, and political power. This gives science an important continuing relationship to democracy, in particular secular democracy—another application

10. Spencer, *Study of Sociology*.
11. Montgomery, "Bias in Interpreting Social Facts," 278–91.
12. Merton, "Science, Technology, and Society," 360–632.
13. Stark, *For the Glory of God*, 123.

of secular methodology which will be taken up in chapter 5. I recognize of course that the secular methodologies of science and government can be, and have been, used by terrible dictators for terrible purposes. But in the end, by using a method which is nonideological, in the long run science will advance most effectively in helpful ways in the free ethos of a democracy. In short, the social sciences are skeptical of the pronouncements and programs of those with power in government and society, a fact which is uncomfortable for, and usually crushed by, autocrats. I believe that in an ethos of freedom, various ideologies (including religious ones) will offset and correct each other. The norms of science contribute to the self-correction of societies. These norms require disinterestedness in the outcome of findings, replication of studies, and public sharing of findings, not to speak of the continual questioning in organized skepticism.

In recent years, as I followed many of the writings of Christian Smith, some of my idealism as a late and enthusiastic convert to secular scientific methodology in the social sciences has been qualified by his strong criticism of his own field of sociology.[14] He shows how social scientists themselves have not escaped the distortions brought about by their own biases. His knowledge of, and experience in, the field is far greater than mine and I recommend becoming acquainted with his criticisms, as well as his useful studies of religion, which have been very helpful to me.[15] Although I share Smith's criticisms of the work of many sociologists, much of which seems to have been under the influence of secularism as an ideology, I found not a few social scientists, such as Smith himself, who demonstrated to me the value of a secular scientific study of human life and who certainly were not anti-Christian. Toward the turn of the century, the field became more moderate in its anti-religious bias because of the common recognition of many sociologists of the importance of religion. One of the ideological views of secularism I noticed, and that Smith identified as quite powerful, was the belief in "individual autonomy."[16] Later, this

---

14. Smith, *Sacred Project of American Sociology*. Smith's use of "sacred" is based on the classic definition of the sacred given by Durkheim in which the sacred is used to define religion. Smith negatively views the sacred project of sociology as what sociologists seek religiously to bring about, thus greatly affecting the scientific value of their work.

15. Among Smith's studies which influenced me are *American Evangelicalism, Moral Believing Animals, The Secular Revolution, Soul Searching, Souls in Transition, Lost in Transition, What is a Person?* and *Religion*.

16. Smith, *Secular Revolution*, 14.

became a major basis for Smith's criticism of fellow sociologists with their "sacred project." He states:[17]

> American sociology as a collective enterprise is at heart committed to the visionary project of *realizing the emancipation, equality, and moral affirmation of all human beings as autonomous, self-directing, individual agents (who should be) out to live their lives as they personally so desire, by constructing their own favored identities, entering and exiting relationships as they choose, and equally enjoying the gratification of experimental, material, and bodily pleasures* [italics his].

As someone on the margin of the social scientific community of scholars I can certainly recognize the influence of this part of the ideology of secularism among sociologists and especially in society at large. However, in light of Smith's own strong recognition of the influence of social structures on individuals, it seems to me that individual autonomy as an ideal even in modern society is moderated by numerous human communities, particularly faith communities. When I lived close to aboriginal societies in Taiwan, I came to recognize that I had a greater sense of autonomy than they had, but nevertheless, I knew myself to be part of a strong faith community which also had a powerful influence on my so-called autonomous decisions. In addition, I believed that the self-destructive nature of living primarily for self-gratification would eventually become fairly evident to most people. I am obviously more of a liberal in various matters than Smith for I believe there needed, and still needs, to be a liberation ("Exodus") for people, such as women and people in the LGBT community, even if the struggle for recognition of their equality leads to some extremism, probably mainly to challenge conventional ideas. I believe LGBT people and women have suffered serious injustices, not to speak of the major oppression and continuing discrimination against African-Americans and other racial-ethnic minorities. It is not surprising that sociologists, some of whom (maybe most) are secularists, as well as others, have felt called to the defense of the marginalized and oppressed and the promotion of "liberty and justice for all." In the end we have the scientific ethos, and especially the specific methods of science, as a protection against some excessive bias in the direction of autonomous individualism in studies and a means of correcting mistaken conclusions. At least that is my belief based on how the secular scientific method is used and the ethos upon which it rests.

17. Smith, *Sacred Project of American Sociology*, 7–8.

While Smith has been quite critical of his fellow sociologists, he also has been critical of Evangelicals, who believe that the Bible is inerrant, emphasizing that those who believe this illogically cannot agree on how to interpret the Bible.[18] Smith, now at Notre Dame University, has moved beyond his original connection with Evangelical Christianity, as distinct from Mainline Christianity, to become a Roman Catholic, explaining the logic behind his move in a book.[19] As I read this book, I realized that he was not talking to me because I and my church do not affirm that the Bible is inerrant, as do many Evangelicals. I believe he considers my Presbyterian Church (USA) as part of "liberal" Christianity, but nevertheless I and many other people have found his scholarship very helpful.

Regarding my choice for personal study through the social sciences, although my graduate dissertation concerned rural-to-urban migration of aboriginal Christians and others in Taiwan, my basic interest was to gain greater understanding of why there had been a large scale movement to Christianity by the aboriginal people among whom I worked in the first place. While making up less than 2 percent of the population of Taiwan, they had become approximately 40 percent of the Presbyterian Church membership. I was amazed having seen the general rejection of Christianity in China as a boy (now after the collapse of Western colonialism, this has greatly changed.). Believing that God works through individual human beings, social forces, and also through historical events and processes, I wanted to see if the social sciences could give me clues as to why the aboriginal people on Taiwan had been so receptive to the gospel. Beyond clues, I wanted to see what social scientific theoretical statements about this might be supported by the evidence. In other words, I thought it would be useful for missiologists and missionaries to have a social scientific theory explaining at least some of the great variations in receptivity to the Christian message. I soon expanded this search for a theory beyond the aboriginals to include the great variations in receptivity to Christianity around the world, but then not only to Christianity. I found that two other religions, Buddhism and Islam, like Christianity, had spread more widely than other religions, but also had been received or rejected in a variety of ways. I still do not understand why missiologists do not seem to have shown much interest in developing theories explaining variations in receptivity to the gospel.

18. Smith, *Bible Made Impossible*, 3–26.
19. Smith, *How to Go from Being*.

This search for theoretical answers (explanations) became the major focus of my research and writing that has continued to the present. However, I usually included the implications I saw for Christian missions in an appendix or the last chapter. Thinking and writing in the social sciences in which the work or action of God is not considered *per se* (only the human reaction or response to what is believed to be God's action) is also why I continued to wrestle with the relationship of the secular to theology. This present brief book is an account of how I have come to understand (so far) the relationship of the secular to thinking and acting, especially to theological thought, and to life in general. I advocate the usefulness of the secular as a methodology in various areas of life where it actually can be an aid to faith. I do not believe that scientific and theological methods can be integrated, as some do, without turning the former into theology and thus implying or claiming that the theological reasoning has become scientific. Trying to integrate the disciplines also removes the scientific work from analysis and evaluation by other scientists. That is why I believe "implications" of scientific findings is a better term for interpreting scientific findings.

Although many intellectuals do not realize or admit it, the historic secularization process in all its complexity was supported by both religious and anti-religious people, as well as many who simply use a secular methodology as a matter of course in everyday life without any sense of challenge to their faith. On the other hand, many conservative Christians feel that their faith is under attack from secularists, perhaps not scientists per se, but secularists who are worshipers of science. I hope to show how a secular approach or methodology—and not only in science, but in other areas as well—can be useful and have positive results for all people, but especially for the life of faith. I am particularly interested in helping Christians clarify their thinking about the secular, how it may be used positively by human beings. Most importantly, Christians should recognize how God is working through secular methodologies to clarify the faith option to believe or not believe in God. I hope that those who may not share the same faith or version of faith with me, or those who have no faith, may see how secular methodology and faith are not antithetical and that the emergence of the secular in the modern era can be a means of clarifying and focusing faith, even if others—both believers and unbelievers—regard it as primarily damaging faith, which it very well may. My viewpoint is that much depends on how secular methodology is viewed and used. Although to me the secular is a mental construct (a type of thinking) and a label used to refer to organizations, activities, and spheres of life that are not specifically religious, I hope to show that the secular as a methodology is actually a useful ally to faith, a major contribution of it being to serve as an important and helpful critic and a means for clarifying faith and reforming Christian communities.

A major goal of the Reformed Christian faith to which I subscribe is that our faith should not only be reformed, but should be continually reforming. One of the most prescient statements ever made by a Christian theologian was referred to in the introduction as the statement made by John Robinson in 1620: "the Lord had more truth and light yet to break forth out of his holy Word."[20] I hope to show that secular methodologies can contribute to the self-reforming task of theology by bringing forth new understandings of what God is doing in the world through human beings.

At this point, my understanding of the secular is that it is a mental construct that may become a virtual obsession with many people so that everything becomes secular, or it may be simply a useful methodology for viewing a world in which nothing is secular (because God is present everywhere and working through all things). Using the secular as a methodology shows a willingness to set aside human ideas about God in order to understand God in the world more fully and to serve God in the world more effectively. Using a secular methodology can actually be made an offering to God and thus become a sacred task.

---

20. Burgess, *John Robinson*, 240.

CHAPTER 2

The Emergence of the Secular

BEFORE PROCEEDING WITH CONSIDERATION of the secular as a methodology in a variety of areas, I am daring to give my version of the emergence of the secular in modern society. In this chapter, I will give reasons for its emergence as being in contrast to what belongs specifically to the religious realm. The term "secular" has Latin origins referring to the temporal, but it was not initially considered a special realm of life in contrast to religious life because all of life, including the temporal, was under the influence of a religious canopy. The secular first came into common use in the church to distinguish between two kinds of religious specialists (clergy) in the church: those who served local parishes or worked "in the world" and were known as secular priests, and those who were members of orders, often living in monasteries or convents, who were known as "the religious," or priests and nuns as opposed to parish priests. In short, "secular" came into use to make a distinction between those working in the temporal or ordinary world of daily life and those who withdraw from the ordinary temporal world, thus becoming more holy or closer to the eternal state of heaven. This distinction continues to be made, particularly in reference to the religious in the Roman Catholic Church, but not generally in Protestant churches, which do not posit a holy status for certain people within the church. I would even question that anything is intrinsically holy except that which is offered up and acceptable to God. Doesn't that make almost everything potentially holy? But the judgment of that is ultimately God's since humans have done many evils in service to God, or as an offering to God.

In traditional societies to this day, people often had no term for religion, primarily because what we call religion permeated life; religious thought and practices were a taken-for-granted part of life. The term "religion" possibly comes from the Latin term, *religio*, meaning to bear a burden. If so, this points to the ordinary concept of religion as primarily a set of obligatory activities or rituals, a sensibility still held by many people. The term "religion" is rarely used in the English Bible, an exception being Jas 1:26 and 27 which reads:

> If anyone thinks they are religious, and do not bridle their tongues but deceive their hearts, their religion is worthless. Religion that is pure and undefiled before God, the Father, is this: to care for orphans and widows in their distress, and to keep themselves unstained by the world.

The Greek term translated here as "religious" and "religion" refers to worship so the passage is a call to worshippers of God to link their worship to carrying out justice in their lives and not following the ways of the world. This of course is a basic message in the Hebrew Scriptures, and James the writer was a respected Jewish Christian. It is actually a characteristic of many religions to separate worship from morality. To take the traditional society of China, the term used for "religion" is expressed by the characters that mean "ancestral" or "traditional teachings." Unfortunately, this tends to emphasize religion as having the right statements of belief in the mind or doing the right rituals, which is a common understanding of many Christians, who then forget to connect their beliefs and religious rituals to carrying out justice.

What is important to know about the difference between modern and traditional societies in regard to religion is that in traditional societies religion was simply an accepted part of life and not something distinguished from a part of life identified as nonreligious, or what we call secular today. Just as there was no special word for religion, there was no special word for the secular. Thus, the secular and religion did not exist as distinct realms in people's thought. They only became distinct realms in the last few centuries in the process of modernization or through the part of modernization called secularization.

The secular mindset is a mental construction that views God as being irrelevant with regard to what is real. This was possible because people realized that nature was distinct though not separate from God's presence. It then became natural to label organizations, institutions, properties, and activities as secular that were neither under the control of religions nor specifically religious themselves. In Europe, these entities were often taken from religious control, and thus secularized. In addition, "secular" came to represent areas of thought separated and freed from the influence (domination according to secularists) of religion or God. Thus the general religious canopy over society was removed or even ripped apart, mainly in the West. The secular came to be understood as being the opposite of religion or of what people believed and practiced based on their ideas of God or the superhuman. This began the struggle to define both the secular and religion, both of which have had to accept multiple definitions. Followers of particular religions often do not consider themselves as followers of a religion, but of the truth of God or of a particular Savior. Believers, such as myself and many others, see their religion as more of a relationship of individuals and communities to God, than as a category or an organized entity. This is especially true of Christians and Muslims. Christians see themselves as followers of Jesus Christ or as those related to God through Jesus Christ. Muslims see themselves as those who are openly submissive to God. Jeffrey Guhin has written of the difficulty in the social sciences of studying religion as a distinct category of behavior.[1] The difficulty is shown by the numerous definitions of religion given by scholars of religion. Nevertheless, a broad working definition can be made, and I believe, contrary to some, it is useful in our modern world where the secular is distinguished from religion in the minds of most people. I also believe that humility requires followers of Christ to recognize themselves as belonging to a religion. Gathering in informal spiritual fellowships seems to be an attempt not to be a religion.

Although many definitions of religion are possible, I find Christian Smith's to be the most comprehensive and useful. He defines it as follows:

> Religion is a complex of culturally prescribed practices based on premises about the existence of the nature of superhuman powers, whether personal or impersonal, which seek to help practitioners gain access to and communicate or align themselves with these powers, in hopes of realizing human goods and avoiding things bad.[2]

The main subject of this book is the secular and so I am not going to enter into a discussion of the various aspects of religion in this definition of religion, but simply make the point that in the modern world people distinguish the secular from religion or what is religious, and the best I or anyone can do is work with that modern understanding and then modify it in various ways. There are many people like myself, as I wrote in the preface and will demonstrate in this book, for whom the secular

1. Guhin, "Religion as Site," 579–93.
2. Smith, *Religion*, 22.

has religious significance as it can be used to serve God. In that sense, I (we) are not modern. But I recognize that the term "secular" is useful to designate organizations, activities, and thoughts that are not specifically labeled "religious" in the terms of the definition just given. An example is secular democracy, which I consider an ideal form of government because in it religions may not use political power to gain adherents and religions become purely voluntary or based on human choice. I believe this is what God wants and therefore I believe secular democracies are the best form of government and are actually in the future for all governments in the flow of history (the Way) as religions have so often been corrupted by political power. That is why secularization movements have been taking place worldwide.

The secular and related terms have been a subject of controversy among social scientists. The related terms to the secular are secularism, secularist, and secularization, and they have all been the subject of an enormous amount of literature. Again, my definition is that the secular is a mental construct and also physical activity in which our idea of God as a causal factor is bracketed out and as such it can be used as a label for whatever is deemed nonreligious. Of course, a believer realizes God is present and therefore offers their thoughts and activities to God, but waits patiently in identifying where God is especially present and active. Regardless of how the secular is defined, in this chapter we consider how we got to where we are in the secularization process or, more accurately, processes, as well as what supports the secular in our society. As already noted, the secular as previously understood was part of church life in the world. After the freedom from religious authority brought about by the Protestant Reformation, combined with nationalistic assertions of power, the scientific movement employing scientific methodologies advanced secular influences. Scientism (the rejection of all knowledge that is not scientifically based) has been the main crutch of secularism. The secular has seemed real because it was based on the reality of nature, but to a believer in God it is not really real beyond a mental construction or even sensibility.

It is important to realize that most early scientists going back to the Middle Ages, and known as "natural philosophers," thought of themselves as learning about God's work through their studies of nature. As science advanced, particularly in the eighteenth and nineteenth centuries, it became clear that its methodology was thoroughly secular. God never comes into scientific reasoning in its description of data or most importantly in its development of theories to explain natural causation. Scientific work became organized or institutionalized first in Italy, where it was suppressed by the Vatican, although Rome earlier and later supported scientific work. Then in the latter part of the seventeenth century, scientific societies were organized in England (Royal Society in 1660) and in France (Academie de Sciences in 1666). This institutionalization of science was accompanied, or at least followed very closely, by concepts of secular democracy based primarily on human rights. The scientific movement was not anti-Christian. However, in the succeeding French Enlightenment of the eighteenth century, an anti-Christian expression of secularization developed most strongly. The Enlightenment, touted by many intellectuals as introducing the modern age, actually rode the wave of new knowledge created by the earlier development of science and rationalistic thought. Furthermore, the leaders of the French Enlightenment and many succeeding intellectuals were actually philosophers and not scientists themselves. They were simply glad to have the opportunity provided by science to challenge religious authority.

By the nineteenth century, the scientific methodology of not attributing any causal factor to God became a new approach to gaining knowledge about the world. In a sense, the secular scientific approach developed naturally as scientists sought to let their natural findings speak for themselves or let the natural patterns be exposed through observation and measurement. This approach affected all other branches of learning and efforts to gain knowledge. As noted, even theology came to use secular methodologies as an aid in interpreting the Bible through analysis of its historical and literary background. This spread of secular methodologies to the study of history (including archeology) and literature, including the Bible, has caused major controversies among Christians, some feeling that this did not show proper respect for the Bible.[3] Biblical criticism was developed, particularly in Germany, and was accepted within the context of faith by many scholars who were considered liberal by conservatives, but also was used destructively by some scholars who were anti-Christian or truly liberal. The work of Darwin and other scientists challenged the view that the Bible was inerrant and should not be interpreted literally,

---

3. Probably the greatest issue for scholars, including Christians, is the resurrection of Jesus Christ. Such an event is practically unknown in normal history; however, strong evidence indicates that Christianity would not have spread except for belief in the resurrection. See Ehrman, *How Jesus Became God*, 6–7. This makes belief in the resurrection of Jesus in the end a matter of faith, which is "normal" for Christian scholars, even though they may use the tools of literary and historical criticism.

particularly in the account of creation. These challenges to the views of a segment of Christians were a major cause for the rise of fundamentalism and the religious right in America. As a result, American Protestantism and Protestantism generally have tended to form into two parties, typically called mainline and evangelical, based on different approaches to, and interpretations of, the Bible, and the resulting different social values. However, I believe my mainline church (Presbyterian Church U.S.A) and most other mainline churches have mostly used biblical criticism wisely with the result of improving interpretations of the Bible.

Thus the early understanding of the secular as a type of work in the church was transformed beginning primarily in the French Enlightenment so that it represented something in contrast with religion, which included anti-religious sentiments or at least views which stood against religious domination. Anti-religious views were more manifest in Europe, but anti-religious domination more manifest in the United States, and anti-religious thinkers rode the wave of the scientific movement with its secular methodology. However, we should recognize that the context for the initiation of modern secularization influences came unintentionally in the challenge to church authority by the Protestant Reformation. This challenge was crucially supported by nationalistic movements. This challenge allowed people to question the domination of the Roman Catholic Church, and later also the Protestant churches, in terms of general knowledge and in political spheres. The effect of the Reformation allowing secularization and being supported by nationalistic movements is often forgotten by theologians and students of the Reformation, who focus only on its theology.

The old unity of the religious canopy over life first began to come apart in Europe before proceeding slowly and uncertainly around the world. The outcome is still uncertain, but it may be quite different from what its early promoters in Europe and also America desired and predicted. If the United States is an example of what may come, religion will not diminish, while at the same time both the values and dangers of secularization will be recognized. The clarification of these dual effects is what this book seeks to contribute to.

Marxism carried the secularization banner, but it has been expressed in the extreme form of making atheism official and has encountered difficulties sustaining itself, particularly after the Soviet Union collapsed.[4]

---

4. See Froese, *Plot to Kill God*, regarding the failure of Soviet experiments in secularization.

In the meantime, religions in China and Cuba are growing in strength in spite of autocratic governments. Russia itself has seen a return to religion, particularly to the mother church of Orthodoxy, not that this is good for democracy. The Muslim world has barely begun the secularization process, but secularization may follow different routes than it did in the West. In Indonesia and Malaysia, perhaps secularization has proceeded the farthest in Muslim majority societies. Although beginning in Turkey in the 1920s and finding expression in Baathist political thought (which involved Christians) and most recently in Tunisia and Egypt in the "Arab Spring," secularization has encountered extreme opposition in the Middle East and its future is still uncertain. In India and Pakistan, secularization is affirmed by political and intellectual leaders, but not practiced by nationalistic populations holding to Hindu and Muslim identities respectfully. In short, the term "secularization" refers to historical processes, most of which are recognized in the West but still take place in many parts of the world. These processes are contested by religious people, but supported by other religious and nonreligious groups who desire freedom of religious and nonreligious thought. Governments and sections of populations support secularization in order to be free from religious domination.

There is still considerable nostalgia for the older religious canopy, represented, for example, in the ideal of the "Christian nation," with its religious trappings, not only in Europe where there are many state churches, but surprisingly even more so in the United States, where an official church is forbidden. Martin Marty described the separation of the secular realm from the religious realm as "the modern schism."[5] He saw it as taking place in three paths: (1) "Towards Utter Secularity: A Clash of Doctrines on the Continent"; (2) "Towards Mere Secularity: 'Everydayishness' in England"; and (3) "Towards Controlled Secularity: Transformed Symbols in America." Although his study is relatively old in the studies of secularization, it appealed to me particularly because it helps us understand the varieties and complexities of secularization and the distinctive approach to it in America. It also seems to capture approaches found on the continent of Europe and in Great Britain.

The French, with their *laïcité*, or laic/cleric antagonism, seem to be the most drastic in their denial of there being any place for religious symbolism, which fits with Marty's view of utter secularity. The various types of secularization help to explain the continuing controversies over its

5. Marty, *Modern Schism*, 18–21; 59–61; 95–96.

meaning and effects. At present, the strongest effects of secularization in terms of detaching people from religion appear to be in Europe, whereas in America secularization seems to have contributed to intensified religious life. Some studies point to America following in the footsteps of Europe, especially among young adults. Many seem disenchanted with the Christian Right, with its leanings toward affirming Christianity as the national religion. Some people seem to suppose this tendency represents Christianity as a whole. In addition, there is a general disenchantment among many people with regard to organized religion. At the same time, there are many vital Christian communities; some are quite large, while at the other extreme, others are small and of the house-church type, or informal startups in restaurants and other nontraditional church settings. The various expressions of religious and secular organizations reflect a major characteristic in Western society of diversity and polarization in religious, social, and political values.

Some of the most enthusiastic followers of secularism (the ideology) advocated and hoped for the fading away of religion. This was a strong cry in the nineteenth century, especially in Europe, and seemed to spring particularly from Enlightenment France and also from Germany, but it was also heard from many academics and writers on both sides of the Atlantic. Reason, rationalism, and especially science were often held up as being the opposite of faith, in spite of the strong participation of Christians in scientific work from the Middle Ages up until that time. Furthermore, many conservative parts of Christianity are quite rationalistic and make greater use of science and technology than older Christian groups. Although the Enlightenment throughout Europe and especially in America was only partly anti-religious, it certainly had the effect of reducing the authority of Christianity or of breaking up the political power of the old religious canopy as church authority and power were reduced. This marked the humiliation of the organized church, which was felt by many Christians to be needed. At any rate, the course of secularization in America proved to be distinct in the way it followed two tracks: religious vitalization combined with loss of religious formal political power. One might add the similar description of the growth and failure of the secular mind, especially among writers and intellectuals, as I understand Robert Coles.[6]

---

6. Coles, *Secular Mind*. In his discussion of the secular mind, Coles also describes two tracks: the growth of the secular mind, especially among writers, as well as the continuing yearning for the sacred.

THE EMERGENCE OF THE SECULAR

Although the founders of the United States respected religion and could be said to have lived under the religious canopy themselves (some have interpreted this to mean that they were highly religious themselves, when they were not), they and their fellow colonists were keenly aware of the misuse of religious power in the old world. It was in the nineteenth century in the United States that religious organizations became major constituents of the larger secular civil society. There was an ever-increasing emphasis on religious choice and religious conversion as opposed to simple assent to a religious faith that had the official approval of the state in a fashion more typical of Europe. This led to the continuation in the nineteenth and twentieth centuries of religious revivals that had begun in the eighteenth century. The religious movements were also manifest in England and the continent in the Pietistic (Germany) or Evangelical (Methodist in England) movements. American religiosity was encouraged by, and fed off of, American individualism, volunteerism, and localism that thrived in the great spaces and opportunities in the New World. The American two-track approach to secularization (opposition to religious domination, but manifestation of widespread religiosity) grew stronger as numerous religiously inspired social movements occurred.

On the continuing strength of religion (the religious track) in America following its founding, Colin Campbell states:

> [T]he secularists in America had to contend with a phenomenon almost unknown to their British counterparts of this period—a vigorous Christian anti-clerical movement. In fact, during the 1820s the Christian anti-clericals had more periodicals in circulation than the free-thinkers—a fact which made it that much harder for the real infidels to mobilize support and which may account for their excessive crudity of approach... Thus, ironically enough, it was the same conditions which appeared to favor the growth of secularism in America which in fact worked against a strong and influential movement.[7]

The nineteenth and twentieth centuries not only contained numerous large- and small-scale religious revivals and movements, but some of the organizations and agencies that were initiated in that time also became social movements. They included the Abolitionist Movement and the Women's Movement, but the most recent one was the most powerful of them all: the Civil Rights Movement. These movements included numerous

---

7. Campbell, *Toward a Sociology of Irreligion*, 59.

domestic and overseas mission movements producing numerous agencies, which represented an enormous investment by religious people in spreading Christianity around the world.[8]

However, looking at the other track in how secularization proceeded, the challenge to the religious canopy came first in politics and then gradually in other fields, particularly in education. Even though the coercive power of government was formally taken away from religion at the nation's founding, a broader secular revolution began to be effective in the United States in many fields by the 1870s and continued well into the twentieth century.[9] The diversity of religions, particularly the different educational approaches of Roman Catholics and Protestants and also among Protestants, caused many leaders in public education to recognize that they had to secularize public education. Formerly, educators had advocated teaching a general Christianity in public schools, but that was identified by Roman Catholics as Protestant Christianity. Even then, although devotionals with Bible reading and prayer in schools were contested as early as the 1880s, they were not taken out of public schools until a Supreme Court ruling in 1962. The reduction or elimination of religious language proceeded over a long time in schools, but also in many other areas such as politics, the legal field, journalism, medicine, and psychology. An often-unrecognized influence in this secularization process in education and other fields is that most general knowledge could be naturally taught and shared from a secular perspective. This will be discussed in chapter 6.

In the general secularization in the public sphere or civil society, the area of life between the private spheres of individuals on the one hand and the government on the other has taken on a secular atmosphere, a kind of political correctness in which references to religion are avoided. This can be seen in the media where journalists tend to be rather ignorant of religions and religious life, and generally avoid mentioning religious groups unless there is some obvious misbehavior! Thus, although churches and other religious volunteer groups remain important participants in civil society, due to the diversity of individual and group religious views, individuals have moderated or even muted their religious language in the public sphere. This is supported by the view that the best witness to faith is in behavior and quality of life, but is sometimes seen by some Christians as fear of openly witnessing or being considered pious. At the same time,

---

8. Wuthnow, *Boundless Faith*.
9. Smith, *Secular Revolution*.

many people express their personal faith, often in a matter-of-fact way, in crisis situations. Furthermore, religious groups are free to advocate for desired government policies and to establish many faith-based institutions and nongovernmental aid organizations. Religious, educational, and welfare organizations are tax free, but political advocacy organizations do not have tax-free status.

The emergence of the modern secular in society can hardly be separated from another process accompanying and supporting the secularization process: the emergence of an ever-increasing emphasis on the autonomous individual. This was expressed especially by intellectuals, many of whom were also writers. As noted in the preface, Christian Smith has called attention to how expressing individual autonomy has even become a special goal of many sociologists.[10] This could be called the most extreme form of autonomy. However, simply because the opportunity to make free choices spread, especially with the Industrial Revolution, the sense of individual autonomy increased. In addition, the open spaces in America offered both individualism and localism as important values. The spread of economic opportunity and the desire for individual rights is also associated with the spread of individualism around the world. Nevertheless, as noted in the preface, extreme autonomy has been moderated by the formation of numerous religious and nonreligious communities and is not as extreme among most people as it is among intellectuals and academics.

The challenge to religious authority and power was made by many individuals in Europe who came to think of themselves as autonomous individuals with freedom to make their own choices. The failures of religion became a favorite subject of intellectuals, who in many respects rivaled or surpassed the authority of religious specialists or leaders (the clergy). For many, especially for those who joined the anti-religious movement, the autonomy of the individual, along with science, became a central value. Even though the autonomy of individuals is upheld by the concept of the rights of individuals as specifically expressed in the Declaration of Independence, paradoxically, these rights were expressed as God-given, that is, it states that "all men [sic]" are "*created* equal" and are "*endowed* by their *Creator* with certain unalienable Rights." The preamble mentions the "Laws of Nature and of Nature's *God*." Thus, whether secularists like it or not, a religious statement was made in the Declaration of Independence, although the Constitution does not mention God. There is a basis, therefore, for qualifying

---

10. Smith, *Sacred Project of American Sociology*.

the full autonomy of individuals by the reference to God in the Declaration of Independence and the mention of "We the people," and promoting the "general welfare" in the Preamble of the Constitution.

If freedom was to be really experienced, then individuals felt they needed to have autonomy from the domination of others and be able to express themselves. Whether autonomy was accompanied by faith was left to personal choice. In this sense, faith became privatized, a fact that has been noted by many scholars of religion. However, this view that faith has become personal and private often overlooks the fact that faith has never been merely private, but has always been a shared experience within religious communities. Personal, yes, but not merely private. It would be more accurate to say that religious faith became both privatized *and* communalized, often on a local and independent, and even an international, basis. Nevertheless, religious groups or churches often have strong national and regional networks and work for common goals, including work overseas, where they maintain many international relationships.[11]

As secularization proceeded in America, the land became filled with very active diverse religious groups. In all cases, great importance was placed on individual choice and this became a key characteristic value of modern Americans. In Christian communities and for many individual Christians, this means making a decision to follow Jesus Christ and a public profession of faith as part of Confirmation after infant baptism or as accompanying baptism. At the same time, the increasing autonomy of individuals means that there are more opportunities for people to reject their own religious heritage or choose another religion or no religion. The latter are the famous "nones" who answer surveys that they have no religion.

A group of scholars, in the book *Rethinking Secularism*, have done the most to clarify the current situation surrounding the phenomenon I am calling "the secular."[12] While there is too much in this book to summarize here, a grasp of the current secular can be gained from the essay in the book by the philosopher Charles Taylor, who earlier authored the large work, *A Secular Age*.[13] As I interpret Taylor, because of all the discussion of the term "secular" based on its history, we are stuck with the term in spite of its ambiguities and the different views of it. This leads me in the next chapter to offer my own approach (influenced by Taylor) to

---

11. Wuthnow, *Boundless Faith*.
12. Calhoun et al., *Rethinking Secularism*.
13. Taylor, "Western Secularity," 31–53.

understanding why we have the secular as an important element in modern thought. Then, beginning with chapter 3, I offer important ways of using the secular by Christians and others. The facts are that the secular has become a part of modern thinking and a way of labeling a variety of entities to distinguish them from what is formally or specifically religious. However, both religious and nonreligious people use the secular and live and work in secular entities, though religious people may regard their work in such entities as sacred.

What has basically happened is that secular thought and activity have become distinct areas of human life and therefore options or choices for human beings to "live in" in America and, increasingly, throughout the world. For some people, this has meant that religion and all that goes with it are virtually irrelevant to them. For many others, a middle position has meant that religion becomes only one aspect of life (it has become compartmentalized) with the rest of life becoming essentially secular. They may grant religion a certain priority in the religious part of their life, but it must take its place alongside of, or in second place to, the practical parts of life, such as making a living, or perhaps a fortune. Nevertheless, for a third type of reaction (the one I favor and seek to promote), faith has taken on deeper meaning as the secular itself is made sacred—surrounded, so to speak, above and below and alongside and even interpenetrated by the presence of God. In this view, the secular becomes primarily a useful methodology for people with faith that is offered up to God in service. Thus, although the contrast between the secular and the religious has been established, an important faith position is to see what is regarded as a secular realm as sacred with God working in and through it. I believe it is this third response, combined with the second, that accounts for the continuing religiosity in America in contrast to where churches have an official status with governments as in Europe.

Conclusion

It is necessary to recognize that secularization processes, together with the rise of individualism, have created a loss of a religious aura that once covered all of life, but the secular way of thought need not be placed simply alongside or above religious thought. From the faith perspective, it is possible to place the secular *within* religious thinking so that both secular and religious thinking come under God. I believe this is done best when secular thinking is treated as a methodology offered up to God. Secular entities or nonreligious organizations, agencies, and institutions can also be seen as a means of service to God. But this placing of secular thinking and entities within a faith perspective requires a specific choice—a choice for God, which becomes the clear faith option to accept God's choice of us to serve God in all things. From a faith perspective is not this the situation a God who wants to be chosen (not hidden from, as in Genesis 3:10) would want? What is important to realize then, is that the rise of the secular does place before human beings as never before the need to make a choice in how life is to be regarded: all under God, only partially under God, or entirely not under God. All three choices are now possible for humans to make as their personal perspective.

CHAPTER 3

Why the Secular Revolution?

BEFORE TURNING TO USEFUL responses to the emergence of the secular, it is worth considering why the secular appeared in a Christian context of all places at a particular point in history. In some ways, the secularization movement (made up of various influences) was inevitable because of the alliance of the church with politically coercive power in the fourth century (the church falling for the temptation that Jesus rejected in the wilderness). This created a basis for challenging the authority of the church, with its obvious failings, particularly in its alliance with political power. At the same time, there were reasons that are inherent in the biblical faith that supported the emergence of the secular. Thus, for reasons which were internal to the biblical faith and external in the reactions of people against the church, the secular emerged as it did in the West. I find the explanation of Charles Taylor, the philosopher, to be the most cogent and satisfying.[1] He identifies three basic reasons to which I give my own elaborations.

Belief that Nature is Distinct from God but Good

An underlying reason for the emergence of the secular is a basic presentation in the Bible of a transcendent creator God who is distinct from the created, good, natural world of which human beings are a part. In other words, because the natural world exists apart from God, it can be imagined as being without the presence of God. Nevertheless, even though the universe is distinct from God, the creator God is working in and through the world that he created ("panentheism"), but this is known only through faith in God. In this thought, nature is not an extension of God or a part of God.

---

1. Taylor, "Western Secularity," 31–53.

This is unlike early and much traditional thought, some of which has been revived by people who think Christianity denigrates nature. The prevailing view in traditional religions saw (sees) nature as part of the divine and hence magical or suffused with spirits, both good and bad. In contrast, the Bible views creation, both animate and inanimate, as distinct from God yet very good and that God made human beings responsible for its care (Gen 2:15). God created nature so that if it is mistreated and damaged, human beings will suffer, but if nature is cared for, there are processes within it that will restore its health. Let me hasten to add that the disenchantment of nature does create the temptation to denigrate and abuse nature. Many environmentalists have said that the biblical doctrine of God giving humans "dominion" over nature (Gen 1:28) encouraged abuse of nature. To offset this temptation is the belief that God requires the tending or tilling and keeping of nature rather than simply dominion of it.

The secular priests working in parishes did not see themselves as working in a world devoid of God's presence, but rather as specializing in working in the temporal sphere in contrast to those working more closely with eternal matters or the holy. Beginning in the Middle Ages, but increasingly after both Reformations, both Roman Catholic and Protestant scholars realized and emphasized that the God of order had created an orderly nature that was ready to be studied so people could learn more about God's wisdom and glory. They discovered the patterns and regularities of nature, but also the exceptions and irregularities with which to compare them. Learning about nature in a systematic way via the scientific movement made it possible to create the technologies that led to the industrial revolution, as well as the means of improving life through modern medical advances. The view that the natural world can be examined and understood rationally was combined with the important experience in the West of forming organizations, especially church congregations.[2] This was important for science since science is basically a group activity. These developments led to the organization and institutionalization of science in the seventeenth century through the Royal Society in England for improving natural knowledge (1660) and the French Academy of Sciences in France (1666) to advance science as was mentioned in chapter 2. The Royal Society was organized by independent, even amateur natural philosophers, and the French Academy by the government. Earlier attempts to organize scientists had taken place

---

2. Huff, *Rise of Early Modern Science*.

in Italy, but this was stopped by the Vatican for a time. Germany followed with a major effort to establish research universities.

Initially, scientists did not feel that they were working in a realm in which God was not present and could not be known. On the contrary, they felt that they were making discoveries about God by reading God's creation. By the next century however, after the institutionalization of science, the fact that people saw creation as distinct from God, a supposition of biblical thought, made it possible for scientists to feel that they could deal with nature apart from God. In the nineteenth century, scientific methodologies became more clearly defined, a process that continued into the twentieth century. These methodologies were entirely secular (as distinct from theological) in that they made no mention of causation by God in the theories they produced. Science became the most clearly secular of the secular methodologies. Both the distinctiveness of creation from God and its goodness made the natural world tremendously attractive as a source of knowledge and also of power as its secrets were uncovered. The rise of technology as an applied science brought amazing results in all areas of life, contributing greatly to the sense of power in human beings apart from God. Unfortunately, given human failings, the power brought by science and its child, technology, meant that along with advances in standards of living and health, enormous destruction was unleashed on the world in the nineteenth and especially the twentieth century. Nevertheless, the results of the secular as a methodology made a great impression on the minds of people and helped to create a category of people who virtually worshipped science and the secular. Thus, the emergence of the secular brought both promise and great danger to human beings. The distinctiveness of God from creation gave humans the realm of nature in which they could choose to live apart from God, or accept nature as a gift from God which they could then offer back in service to God and others. Theologically speaking, this was one of the great risks of God in creating a reality separate from God's self.

Belief in the Creation of an Inner New Life

This reason for the emergence of the secular was unexpected to me. The Bible emphasizes the inner life of individuals. The New Testament especially emphasizes the creation of a new inner person. The church maintained this emphasis, but the church also became a victim of its own success by becoming an established institution closely allied with the state, falling for the temptation that Jesus rejected. Mystics, monks, and nuns ("religious virtuosi") gave special attention to the inner life, but for large numbers, believing became primarily assent to church teachings and outward conformity, rather than a personal and inner commitment. A natural tendency of human beings has been to emphasize the materiality of life in contrast to the spiritual life. People feel trapped in life's materiality and need or want to escape it. However, the biblical emphasis is that the inner and outer life is to be coordinated so that the inner life is not subject to the outer life, but the outer life follows the lead of the inner life as an expression of inner faith. The apostle Paul declares, "So we do not lose heart. Even though our outer nature is wasting away, our inner nature is being renewed day by day" (2 Cor 4:16). (At 88, this is one of my favorite verses!)

Charles Taylor states, "Now, a striking feature of the Western march toward secularity is that it has been interwoven from the start with this drive toward a personal religion, as has frequently been remarked."[3] In the High Middle Ages, there was a growth of Christocentric religion. Taylor describes the subsequent development of personal religion:

> From that point on, the pressure to adopt a more personal, committed, and inward form of religion continues—through the preaching of the mendicant friars and others, through the devotional movements mentioned above—eventually reaching a new stage with the Reformation. The point of declaring that salvation comes through faith was radically to devalue ritual and external practice in favor of inner acknowledgment of Christ as savior. It was not just that external ritual was of no effect, but relying on it was tantamount to a presumption that we could control God. The Reformation also tended to delegitimize the distinction between fully committed believers and other, less devoted ones . . . All Christians were expected to be fully committed.[4]

Following the Protestant Reformation and in the midst of the religious wars in Europe of the sixteenth and seventeenth centuries, there was a return by Protestants (in contrast to an earlier more dynamic faith expression) to a scholastic emphasis on believing (accepting) correct doctrine, or orthodoxy. The creed to which people outwardly subscribed became a matter of life or death for many. Many confessional statements were written

---

3. Taylor, "Western Secularity," 38.
4. Ibid., 37.

to become the basis for both personal and national identities. However, the wars of religion that ended with the Peace of Westphalia in 1648 (settling religious identities of many nations) were followed by the renewal of inner faith in the Evangelical and Pietist Movements in the eighteenth and nineteenth centuries—the latter primarily in Germany and the former primarily in England and extending to the United States. The recent adoption of the evangelical label as an alternative name to fundamentalists for nonmainline Protestant church Christians is an attempt to claim continuity with eighteenth- and nineteenth-century evangelicals. There is partial justification in this, but nineteenth-century evangelicals (in reaction to the injustices of the Industrial Revolution) placed greater emphasis on social justice. The continuity for recent evangelicals exists in the emphasis on the inner life of faith, which became almost an exclusive emphasis of recent evangelicals (like fundamentalists) to the near exclusion of social justice.

At any rate, beginning at least in the eighteenth century, Protestants gave a new emphasis to the inner personal life of faith as being more important than simply believing a formal creed. Those emphasizing the Enlightenment of this period often overlook this contemporary religious movement and its major impact on the world. In the United States, where formal separation of church and state was intended to protect personal faith, the religious movements of the eighteenth and especially the nineteenth centuries gave added emphasis to individual personal faith. This led in the twentieth century to fundamentalists—reacting to mainline churches—not placing a corresponding emphasis on the importance of Christian community and unity.

The call for an individual choice to believe (being "born again") helped to emphasize the distinction between the transcendent and immanent alongside the spiritual and material spheres. The immanent or material sphere then became free in people's minds to be regarded as separate from religion and therefore secular, even though in the life of faith both spheres were in God's domain. Thus the sacred canopy was broken even more than earlier except for the eyes of faith, namely for those accepting the faith option to believe in God's choice of us, as I indicated in the preface. Without the eyes of faith, only the secular sphere remained for many, but even with the eyes of faith it was a temptation to separate spiritual and secular life, the latter to be dealt with practically. The three positions mentioned at the end of the previous chapter then appeared. First, for some, the secular in the form of science and the autonomous individual became a realm free from God so that science, the individual, and the material alternated as gods. Second, another position appeared for some, perhaps many, religious people: living in two realms—the realm of religion, in which faith was operative, and the secular realm, where ordinary practical knowledge was operative. And finally, some religious people, whether a majority or not, were challenged to accept the path of comprehensive faith—living simultaneously in both the religious and secular realms by sensing, seeing, and serving God in the world and continually offering their lives and activities in it up to God. Perhaps many of us Christians and people of other faiths alternate between the second and third positions. Nevertheless, seeking to follow the third path means accepting the challenge to improve, correct, and grow in and by the secular realm made sacred under God as the life of faith matures. It is the path I would like to follow and that I am hoping to promote with this book. This requires humbly acknowledging that one's religious ideas are partial and incomplete.

Christian Failures

The first two reasons for the emergence of the secular were inherent in biblical faith, which glorified nature, not as God, but as God's creation, and also distinguished the inner and outer life with faith arising from the inner life leaving the outer life (perhaps unintentionally) to be dominated by the secular. However, the secularization movement that appeared in the West also contained a clear anti-Christian element that was in response to the Christianity that many saw and knew. In the end, I believe the failures of Christianity dating initially from its alliance with the coercive power of the state in the fourth century did much to generate the anti-Christian response within the secularization movement. Thus, in addition to the belief positions—belief in the distinction of God from nature or the transcendent from the immanent, and belief in the importance of the inner life of religion contrasting with the outer life—the authoritarianism of Christianity created a reaction against it. This authoritarianism gave Christianity a tendency to be associated with coercion and war. Coercive force then combined with institutionalism, which sat in contrast to the movement-centered spirit of the church, which was manifest in the spread of the gospel, first in the Mediterranean world and then in Europe. All of this contributed greatly to the weakening of the church's social and political influence and to its becoming irrelevant to many. Institutionalization is a necessary human process following movements, but it has been difficult for the church to overcome its weakening effect on the life of faith as outward conformity has become more important than inner faith.

Throughout history, rulers have typically used religion as a means of social control by making it a unifying ideology for the people. In addition, since rulers need to be legitimized (to avoid having to rule by force alone) they obtained their desired authority from religions that they then made official and monopolistic. Religions, for their part, welcomed receiving the support of governmental authorities and becoming monopolistic. I call this the marriage made in hell. This pattern has great appeal to many rulers and religious leaders and continues in the world. The nation-state of Israel, in the Hebrew Scriptures and up through New Testament times, attempted to combine faith with a nation and it became a failed nation before the time of Jesus Christ. The last attempt in ancient history to combine the faith of Israel with a nation was the Hasmonean kingdom, which lasted approximately 100 years. This was followed by successive attempts to establish a kingdom in the rebellions against Rome that led to the destruction of the temple and final expulsion from the land. In spite of these repeated failures, the faith of Israel survived because of the inner reality of the faith of the Jews simply in being God's people, chosen by God whatever circumstances they may be in or wherever in the world they might live.

Jesus very clearly rejected the alliance of his Way with coercive power from the beginning of his ministry, as seen in his rejection of the temptations in the wilderness, and climaxing in his death on the cross followed by his resurrection. Furthermore, Jesus and his followers made no claim to, and had no interest in, establishing a territorial kingdom. Apocalyptic Jews and Christians continue to have interest in a territorial kingdom and thereby distort the meaning of "inherit the earth," (Ps 37:9–11; Matt 5:5) or true ownership of the earth and anything and everything in it. It also distorts the apocalyptic thought that is primarily meant to comfort by portraying a triumphant God and the temporary nature of earthly power, and instead uses the highly symbolic destructive language of apocalyptic thought to justify earthly wars.

In the fourth century, in accordance with the age-old practice of religions and governments, the state and the Christian church made their fateful alliance. Thus the church followed the path of ancient Israel. By its alliance with political power, the Christian church became increasingly authoritarian, assuming special prerogatives over political entities and overall domination over knowledge and politics that lasted for centuries. The vestiges of it are still present in the favoritism of governments to particular churches. The church became both a religious and a secular power. In subsequent centuries, various movements, such as the Franciscans, Dominicans, Jesuits, and others, sought to revive and increase the spiritual life of the church. They were co-opted as orders within the church, thus strengthening the concept of the religious as being holier than ordinary Christians. Opposition to the power of the Orthodox Church based in Constantinople that developed in churches in the Middle East was expressed in the iconoclastic controversy, but also in different interpretations of creedal statements. This prepared the ground for the Islamic movement. In the West, strong opposition movements to church authority and power appeared in the Middle Ages, such as the Bogomils in the Balkans, Cathars or Albigenseans in southern France, Waldensians, Lollards, and Hussites, but these (except for the Waldensians) were all crushed, even though the latter three were more orthodox than the former ones who were extremely dualistic—an attempt to emphasize the spiritual life over the worldliness of the church. Finally, in the sixteenth century, the Protestant Reformation successfully challenged the authority of the Roman Catholic Church, but only with the crucial backing of nationalistic movements in Germany, France, England, Scotland, Holland, and Scandinavia. The radical Protestants, determined to make a clear distinction between church and state, were persecuted by other Protestants and Roman Catholics. Terrible religious wars followed for almost a century and a half. These have remained a major point for criticism from within the secularization movement. (Who wants such cruel religions?!) As noted, the Peace of Westphalia in 1648 settled which church, Roman Catholic or Protestant, would be the dominant church in various European countries. However, the alliance between Christianity and political power continued, following the common assumption of both Roman Catholics and Protestants that each nation needed to have a single or dominant religion or state religion. The age of scholastic orthodoxy and the creation of many confessions of faith exacerbated authoritarianism in Christianity and its institutionalism, and likewise exacerbated reaction to it in secularization.

The centuries leading up to the eighteenth-century Enlightenment had revealed that the authority of churches could be successfully challenged, but this was not enough. The good side of this challenge is that the nature of religious authority began to be clarified. That is, the attempt of the church both to dominate governments and to control knowledge was shown to lead to the misrule of governments and result in false and harmful knowledge. This nature of the church's authority and of spiritual power is still being clarified. What does Jesus' claim to absolute authority mean (Matt 28:18)? Gradually, nation-states discovered that they did not need religious approval, at least from a single religious body, and this was formalized in the new setting of the United States, the place to where diverse ethnicities and religious groups had migrated and continued to migrate in an accident of history, which I believe was providential. The struggle to understand how to relate religion to governmental power continues with many governments and people discovering freedom from religious domination.

Initially, the challenge to the authority of the church was made possible on an intellectual level by the new emphasis on the Bible as the source of authority for matters of faith. This raised the individual conscience (mentioned above in the second reason for secularization) to a place of authority over secular power. As noted, the challenge to religious authority, which was accompanied by state power, could not have succeeded when it did without the support of secular power in the form of nationalistic governments. In some ways, the Protestant movement became tied to national powers and nationalism, much as the older churches (Orthodox and Roman Catholic) became tied to imperial powers. Whatever the case, it is clear that geopolitical forces definitely had, and still have, an influence on religious developments, as seen most lately in the collapse of Western colonial power and the leveling of national powers, which has been accompanied by the explosive growth of Christianity, especially in Africa and China. The movement for nations to cooperate, as expressed in the United Nations and numerous international agreements, has just begun even though it is opposed by nationalistic Christians with other ultranationalists. At present, Christian churches have largely lost their power over, but not their influence on, governments. The responsibilities of governments toward their people and the world continues to be an important part of theological thought and attempts to influence government policies and programs continue to be considered a Christian responsibility, but Christians disagree on what those policies and programs should be. What remains important for most people is both religious and political freedom, the first being freedom to worship and propagate the faith, and the latter being freedom of the people to form governments responsible to them and freedom of governments to be free from religious control.

Further failings of Christianity are seen when looking at technological developments based on the scientific movement. Technological developments greatly spurred the Industrial Revolution that spread from England throughout Europe and to the United States, and in the last century, to most of the world. However, the Industrial Revolution, while raising the standard of living for many, brought great suffering to many others. Religious bodies initially seemed detached from this suffering and not a few continue to be detached as they focus on the spiritual life. The many injustices that were tolerated by Christendom during the Industrial Revolution in Europe and later in America further stimulated rejection of Christianity. The antireligious secularized people found a great moral cause in the call to bring justice to the suffering laborers in societies. It is highly significant that the Marxist and Communist movement that made atheism an official part of its ideology and saw religion as an enemy, arose in the context of what was considered Western Christendom. Others, less radical than Marxists, felt (and still feel) that religion in general, and particularly conservative religious groups, have brought harm to societies by not advocating progressive reforms and even supporting businesses and industrial practices that oppress people and damage the environment. Adding to the criticism of Christianity is the opposition of some Christians to science and its efforts to understand changes in the environment. Beyond that, the association of religious groups with hawkish military positions, coupled with extreme nationalism that rejects international cooperation, continues to fuel anti-Christian attitudes and therefore the ideology of secularism.

Conclusion

Clearly the causes for the secularization process are complicated and may be traced to both inherent theological reasons and religious failure causes. Furthermore, it should not be forgotten that Christians, as well as anti-Christians promoted secularization, desiring freedom from other religious domination. Thus, secularization processes and influences should not be seen as entirely bad. An overall effect of secularization may be termed the necessary humiliation of Christianity and of religion in general, which has been needed even if it has been carried too far in some quarters and areas. Certainly the church lost power and influence in the West, but also in areas where Marxism has spread to non-Western countries. Christianity has been humiliated and demoted from its days of domination over societies and nation-states. At the same time, the forces promoting secularization have had their failures, most notably in the loss of power and influence of Communism and the failure of "the plot to kill God."[5] Furthermore, paradoxically, in the United States, where religion was formally demoted from an official position, religion continued (and still continues) as a vital force in individuals and communities. Thus, humiliation of the church in the overall secularization process has benefited the church in bringing it closer to the lives of many people. Nevertheless, problems remain for the church as there seems to be a turning away from organized religion as increased numbers in the West (not in many non-Western countries) declare that they have no religion (the "nones"), especially young adults. With this background on the emergence of the secular, I turn to a consideration of at least five areas where there can be positive uses of the secular in the form of methodologies that may be applied to various aspects of life. These methodologies point to how the secular can protect and strengthen religion and why religion needs to respect and make valuable use of the secular as a methodology, even while recognizing its dangers.

I do not expect complete agreement with me on the meaning of the secular and its related terms, but I trust there can be at least enough agreement for people to follow my reasoning regarding the secular. As I advanced in my studies in sociology of religion, I discovered that there was considerable interest and much disagreement and debate among sociologists of religion and other scholars about the secular, especially secularism and the movement they identified as secularization. This debate also included the projected course of secularization, some assuming that religion would be passing away or at least becoming a minor influence in life. What is especially interesting is that at present, at the beginning of the twenty-first century, there is among sociologists of religion and historians a reconsideration of earlier views in which religion was believed to be diminishing in the face of the expansion of the secular realm, or all that is labeled secular, and the thought about it. Increasing numbers of scholars now realize that religious thought and activity continue to be widespread throughout the world, though some of it, unfortunately, is supportive of violence. Religiously fueled violence among Muslim groups plagues the Middle East, just as violence between Christian groups plagued Western Europe in the sixteenth and seventeenth centuries, and even more recently in Northern Ireland, not to mention the contemporary violent groups of

---

5. Froese, *Plot to Kill God*.

racists claiming to be Christian. However, some scholars have recognized that the secularization process itself has brought about a focus on personal and communal religion. Paradoxically, instead of being eliminated, religion has been deepened and spread.[6]

My conclusion about the secularization processes is that the emergence of the secular as a mindset or construct of the mind and a recognized way of labeling that which is not formally religious, does not require the discarding of faith, but quite the opposite. Nevertheless, many have rejected religion by becoming followers of secular*ism*. Secularism refers to a universalizing of the secular mental construct so that nothing beyond the secular sphere is considered real, whereas for the believer the secular itself (the mindset) does not have ontological reality. In contrast, the secular mindset sees faith itself as being based on an illusion. In this way, the secular method is turned into a philosophy and also a style of life in which God is considered irrelevant, even unreal. The secular becomes an idol, making secularism a form of idolatry. I would add that religious concepts and practices can also become idolatrous. The tangible gods of secularism are usually science with the addition of the autonomous self that thrives in the freedom brought by the reduction or removal of religious authority. Smith describes the exaggerated concept of individual autonomy.[7] Scientism is quite close to secularism in that science can be universalized as the sole source of reliable knowledge and made into a substitute for God.

People of faith consider that there is important theological knowledge of reality existing beyond the natural realm, even though it is not subject to scientific examination. Furthermore, this reality beyond the natural realm is a reality to which we are led by God's self, who intruded into or invaded the world, particularly human life and history. This makes the three biblically related religions who believe this—Judaism, Christianity, and Islam—apocalyptic religions, apocalypse meaning "unveiling" or "revelation." Theology must interpret this revelation, both its meaning and its content. This theological knowledge is relevant to how to relate to and use the secular, as we shall see in the chapters which discuss the secular as offering various useful methodologies for people of faith, as well as everyone else.

---

6. Beck, *God of One's Own*; Joas, *Faith as an Option*; Coles' book, *The Secular Mind*, may be seen as showing the failures of the secular for many people.

7. Smith, *Secular Revolution*, 43–45; *Sacred Project of American Sociology*, 7, 8.

CHAPTER 4

Secular Methodology in Science

As I mentioned in the introduction, my approach will be personal and illustrative of the various secular methodologies that I have observed and experienced, beginning with the social sciences. In the area of social sciences, my training and experience has been in social scientific studies of religion. My struggle with the relationship of the secular to my theology—which is still going on—began with my encounter with the secular methodology of the social sciences, especially in studying religion, which of course is not purely secular. I am certainly not a natural scientist or highly advanced in scientific thought as used in mathematics and physics, but it is not necessary to be a scientist of any type to recognize the value of the secular methodology in science.

There are many fields within science (both natural and social science), but I believe the sociology of religion within the social sciences encounters theological concerns most often, even though the encounter of theology with biology and evolution has received the most publicity. This is because of its different account of creation from Genesis, which requires that Genesis be interpreted theologically rather than literally. That is not surprising to most Christian scholars except for vocal fundamentalists. Social scientists introduced me to the secular methodology of science in courses on research methodology and statistics. They wanted to make sure I knew that they regarded the social sciences as science, in spite of what some might think.

The purpose of this chapter is not to describe formal scientific methodology, which incorporates many different techniques that are described in books and courses on research, but to emphasize its secularity as I soon discovered it in my graduate school program in social scientific studies of religion. Although I did not advance far in statistics, I discovered the important fact that statistics was simply formalized and systematic common thought. I believe scientific methodology forms a model for all analytic thought, which I consider thought that looks for causal relationships and is not simply descriptive or narration. The fact is, we constantly think in terms of probabilities and we make generalizations from our mental sampling of observations, which may or may not be representative of populations. If we think analytically, we even conduct simulated mental experiments with experimental and control groups in making comparisons. This enables us to understand general trends, at least to some extent. I have come to think that a course in statistics is useful for anyone, perhaps especially including theologians, church historians, and other church leaders, in order to stimulate objective and analytical thought.

The clearest use of the secular in the modern era has been as a methodology for science. In many ways, because of its clear secular approach, science led the way in secularization processes, with secularists continually pointing to science as the only reliable source of knowledge. "I won't believe in God unless God is proven to me" is actually a very old natural human viewpoint expressed by those looking for a sign like Thomas in John 4:24–29. However, as noted before, science was not so clearly secular to the early scientists. The earliest scientists (natural philosophers) in the European Middle Ages, and the ones at the time of the institutionalization of science in the seventeenth century, saw their work as learning about the ways of God in nature. However, it became evident as time passed that scientific work did not require any reference to God since nature exists distinct from God. God's presence and work in the world and in nature is only known by faith. In fact no cause in nature, including human life and especially religion, was to be attributed to God in scientific studies. If one is studying religion, only the human belief in God (not actually God) or the human side of religion (not actually action from God), could be considered a causative factor. Nevertheless, as the sociologist Rodney Stark pointed out, Christianity was essential for the initiation of the scientific movement because of the doctrine of a rational God, not an arbitrary divinity, who created an orderly, not a chaotic, universe.[1] In other words, he pointedly saw religious faith as a causative force in the development of science. In this sense, science really rests on normative assumptions and, as we have seen, the ethos of scientific work includes normative expectations of scientists.[2]

1. Stark, *For the Glory of God*, 123.
2. See pages 3 to 4 in Chapter 1 in this book, and Merton, "Normative Structure of

Beyond that, in comparing Chinese, Islamic, and Western science, Toby Huff pointed out that the experience in Western Christianity and society of forming legal corporations—and, I would add, experience in congregations—led to the successful organization of scientific work.[3] Scientific work or advancement is essentially a group activity, as research universities and centers demonstrate. It turned out that science would advance in the West because science advanced best, not as the individual activity of geniuses, but as an organized group activity. Thus science became institutionalized, as noted earlier in the seventeenth century in England and France. In the subsequent centuries, science advanced rapidly and spread throughout Europe and the rest of the world.

Evidence systematically gathered from the natural world stands on its own in scientific descriptions and theory. However, as noted, people, including scientists, often forget that there is one aspect of scientific study that is not scientific: the choice of what to study is made on a normative or biased basis in the technical meaning of bias, namely personal interest with its limited perspective. I like to point out that the importance of opinion and choice in human life is inescapable, including even in science, which blows a hole in many peoples' vaunted opinion of science, including scientists themselves. As noted in chapter 1 and in my article, according to the early social scientist Herbert Spencer, all people are biased.[4] People are often motivated to study a subject of personal interest or to follow a research agenda that is established by an organization with a particular interest. Often a motive may be to clarify, elaborate, or disprove an already widely accepted theory. People may well desire to establish a new theory in an unexplored area, perhaps to make a name for themselves or perhaps to provide a basis for aid to people through some technological advance. Motives are usually mixed. My reason for trying to develop a theory of the spread of religions was based primarily on my personal experience of seeing great variations in how Christianity and then other religions have spread. I wanted to clarify why this was so and then be able to promote good policies for spreading Christianity. This is far from a scientific motive, but after establishing my goal I undertook study by methods that were secular and as scientific as I could make them.

Science," 267–78.

3. Huff, *Rise of Early Modern Science*, 148.

4. Spencer, *Study of Sociology*; Montgomery, "Bias in Interpreting Social Facts," 278–91.

Many scientists are reluctant to recognize their personal motivations or even that science rests on a set of normative assumptions and that it operates within a set of norms that forms its ethos. Christian Smith made clear some of the biases found in many sociological studies to support liberal or progressive social and political goals.[5] I believe the normative basis for science, not necessarily the normative basis of particular studies, is very important for its connection to freedom and democracy, in which there is freedom to question authority, particularly to speak truth to power. Nevertheless, science as a whole, and in its specific work, is essentially a secular discipline, even though I believe the normative assumptions it rests upon are very consistent with Christian beliefs and values and were originally inspired by them.

As a Christian, I especially appreciate the humble strength of the sciences based on the fact that they have to be subject to review, replication, and correction by subsequent studies. This explains my bias favoring scientific studies because I think science has a built-in basis for humility since its findings are tested. In contrast, the arts almost require non-humble assertions of personal opinions that cannot be tested, but are only subject to agreement or disagreement. Of course the arts speak to an emotional side of life which is very important for life fulfillment. Theology shares to some extent with the arts a strong place for emotion, with the key difference that agreement on the theological views of faith is the basis for historic communities of faith. It is even true that particular communities or denominations share similar cultural characteristics, for example in their liturgy, their music, the language typically used, and even similar material expressions in buildings and art. In many ways, I believe that the scientific approach has done much to make scholarship, including theological scholarship, more humble. At the same time, human beings have to live by their norms and opinions and the world basically knows that. There are even denominations or schools of thought among both secular scientific and nonscientific scholars.

The natural sciences developed before the social sciences, and to this day when the term "science" is used, people often think primarily of the natural sciences. The findings and theories developed in the natural sciences have had a dramatic effect in societies, particularly as they have contributed to the development of technologies benefiting many people. Technologies in industry and scientific medicine made great advances

---

5. Smith, *Sacred Project of American Sociology*.

benefiting human life largely based on scientific study and work. Of course, scientific work has produced knowledge and technology that has been used to harm people, but all the advances in knowledge and technology (in spite of the "mad scientists") have given science enormous prestige. The many fields in science and technology have lifted standards of living around the world. It is no wonder that science—and the secular with it—has attracted so many worshippers, beginning with the French Enlightenment! In many ways, science has replaced nature, its object of study, as an object of worship. Nevertheless, even in the present, many questions are being raised about the potential harmful effect on people of communication technology, including social media, photographic possibilities, artificial intelligence, and the construction of virtual reality and robots.

Science started, but did not stop, with investigations of nature. Because of my concentration in the social sciences, I point out that in the centuries following the development of the natural sciences, and even to some extent at the same time, secular methodologies were increasingly applied to the study of human behavior beginning with politics and economics, for example in the writings of Machiavelli (1469-1527) and Adam Smith (1723-1790). However, especially in the nineteenth century, the secular scientific approach was applied increasingly to the study of human behavior in the fields of psychology, economics, political science, anthropology, and sociology. These became known as the social sciences or sometimes the behavioral sciences by the twentieth century. Being called "the soft sciences" is somewhat justified because data about human thought and behavior are more malleable and difficult to examine than in controlled studies of rocks and trees or stars and planets. Theories are naturally more difficult to establish in the social sciences than in the natural sciences (where they are difficult enough). Some may not even consider the social sciences to be real sciences. Nevertheless, the various social sciences are well established fields of study with departments in most universities. They each have century-old member associations, produce many publications, and maintain professional ladders. Anthropology and sociology are often grouped together in college departments, but unfortunately in the United States (not so much in Europe) they have become divided disciplines, primarily because of different research histories—anthropologists tending to study villages and small groups, and sociologists tending to study urban areas and large populations, often employing statistical methods of analysis. I noticed the rivalry of these disciplines in graduate school and yet found value in each for explaining religious change. My purpose here is to make the point that the whole scientific approach may be termed secular or nonreligious, which places it in contrast to religious thought or the approach of theology. Uncovering causes (developing a theory) is a basic purpose of both the natural and social sciences, which is what attracted me to them because I was looking for reasons for variations in response to outside religions. However, I believed it was important to maintain the distinction between secular and theological approaches, which I found was often not maintained by scholars in my theological field of interest: missiology.

One of the important distinctions in science that I find least recognized among nonscientists is the distinction between description and explanation, otherwise known as theory. Although description is important for exploratory purposes and is often quite interesting (more than theories which are necessarily abstract) and important for making classifications or distinguishing types of behavior, the basic purpose of science is to develop theory or explanation. This consists primarily of understanding relationships between facts or phenomena—hopefully causal relationships—although they may only be correlations. Descriptions are often available through historical studies and literature of various types that go more deeply into human nature (which makes them more interesting than much science), yet theory construction remains the goal of science.

I have not mentioned the centrality of the empirical, but all scientific studies, whether in the natural or social sciences, pay great attention to the empirical, namely to what is observable and measurable in some way, and the experienced. Although many aspects of human life are not directly observable—such as the inner aspects of human life which are expressed or seen in values, attitudes, motivations, and all kinds of emotions—they are very important in the social sciences and can be studied through empirical indicators. One thing was clear to me from the beginning of my study: social scientists consider themselves scientists and their use of scientific methodologies was thoroughly secular. However, the emphasis on empiricism or positivism has been carried too far in science, especially social science, so that now there are social scientists doing promising work in advancing the approach of critical realism combined with personalism. I first encountered this in the writings of Smith.[6] Although I am still seeking understanding of this approach, I recognize that it is opposed to the extreme empiricism

---

6. Smith, *What is a Person*, 90–115. He also includes a discussion of "antiscientistic phenomenology."

(positivism) of some social scientists. As I understand it, the approach of critical realism is to recognize the reality of causes beyond the empirical and material and also beyond our human consciousness. I like the attention critical realism gives to what is actual and to causes that exist within the structures and capacities of societies. As Smith says, "not everything that is real is observable, since reality possesses a 'deep' dimension operating below the surface of direct human apprehension."[7] This is far from a real introduction to critical realism, but I believe its approach holds promise to make social scientific studies come closer to reality in their theories.

I must admit that as a late convert to social scientific study, I probably overestimated its contribution to knowledge. Although "journalistic" and "anecdotal" are pejorative terms in the social sciences, I have found over the years and especially lately that journalists and people with extensive experience in government service around the world can create important knowledge by describing inner states of mind through narratives that give a more realistic and in-depth sense of a situation in a social and political development than is possible (or can be afforded) in most social scientific studies. At times I have found social scientific studies seemingly trivial, although an argument can be made that an accumulation of highly focused studies is needed on many subjects. Inevitably it is almost necessary to specialize on a subject of personal interest and this is what I have tried to do in focusing on the spread of religions. In addition to the work of journalists and experienced government and nongovernmental workers (especially those with overseas experience), I found that scholars in the humanities have contributed much general knowledge about human behavior. This applies especially to the work of historians with their use of materials from original sources and also their narrative accounts and biographies. Literature of various kinds—such as novels, poetry, and accounts of imaginary events, sometimes using metaphorical or symbolic language—delve into the inner states of persons and give a sense of conditions not given in the social sciences. This certainly applies to the Bible! Historical accounts and various types of literature provide important data that often stimulates and inspires systematic social scientific studies. Philosophy—as seen in the philosophical concept of critical realism and other concepts of reality—can inspire social scientists to incorporate new perspectives in studying the social realities they encounter.

---

7. Ibid., 95.

At the same time, scientific methodology, with its systematic and secular approach, especially in its attempts at maintaining objectivity (control for bias), has influenced the humanities with its many branches. This includes—especially of concern for Christians—the Christian and non-Christian academic studies regarding how to interpret the Bible. Secular historical and literary critical studies have greatly aided interpretation of the Bible. It is important, however, to keep in mind that interpretation of the Bible involves more than these secular studies, as helpful as these are, and must employ a theological perspective that keeps in mind how language, events, and activities all point beyond themselves to ultimate realities beyond the natural world. One of the major positions for theology is that theological affirmations and assertions can be, and are, made without fear of contradiction because theological statements are not subject to empirical or experimental verification, as are all scientific theories. The result, of course, is the creation of numerous religious groups having various interpretations of the Bible. A basic fact, however, is that science cannot be used to establish important theological beliefs, even though a secular study may point toward them. For example, I think of Bart Ehrman's view that Christianity cannot be explained without the strong belief of the early followers in the resurrection of Jesus Christ.[8] He certainly uses a secular historical approach and does not believe in the resurrection in the same way as I do, but he does recognize the power of the belief in the resurrection. I believe it is very difficult for nonbelievers (and believers) to explain the widespread belief in the resurrection, although Ehrman tries.

One of the issues for Christians in a critical approach to the Bible is the tendency of some scholars, such as Ehrman, to deny most, if not all, supernatural events reported in the Bible. But this has not been a major issue for me as I will briefly explain. Regarding beliefs which are not provable (though not disprovable either) through scientific methods, I regard the greatest supernatural event in history as the incarnation of God seen in God as a baby, God among people, and God on a cross so that we could be redeemed from an old life to a new life. Belief in the resurrection is almost an obvious outcome of such a life and death. This may be extended to many other "not normal" events in the Bible. It is from following Jesus out of love for him and his Way that faith in his resurrection is finally based. In that regard, I believe it is important that Jesus did not try to establish belief in his resurrection by appearing to those responsible for his crucifixion,

---

8. Ehrman, *How Jesus Became God*, 204.

which would have scared them into believing in his physical resurrection. A reaction would have been to want to replicate resurrection for their soldiers, depending on which side they were on, to crush Rome's enemies or to win freedom from Rome. I like to point out that Jesus did not work any miracles of healing on his disciples and in the case of Paul, specifically did not bring healing for his physical ailment, perhaps bad eyes.

I have come to believe that much theology is a matter of emphasis, the central one for Christianity being love and aiming at following Jesus Christ, the ultimate authority for life. Thus, because I believe in God's interference in history, especially in Jesus Christ, I feel free to use studies of the Bible by those who do not believe in this interference to see what insights they may have regarding the human aspects of the Bible. Unfortunately, many Christians exhibit a docetic tendency in approaching the study of the Bible, just as they do regarding Jesus Christ. Docetism was the tendency of some early Christians not to accept the full humanity of Christ.

Basically, I believe it is important for theological and scientific thought to be clearly distinguished, although the barrier between them is something like a one-way looking glass. This is because scientific thought cannot include any theological reasoning, but theological thought needs to view and incorporate valid scientific findings and theories. Thus, theological thought—like philosophy, its sibling—is more comprehensive because it must incorporate all reality, both of nature and beyond nature, whereas science can only deal with natural realities or reality with empirical indicators, such as for the inner life of human beings. However, through the use of the approach of critical realism, social scientists are seeing reality in larger and deeper terms than only as empirical data. Also, it is important to keep in mind that scientific study might be motivated by a normative concern, such as revealing causes for unjust social conditions or disproving a religious viewpoint. However, once a subject for scientific investigation is chosen for normative reasons, including theological reasons, the actual study must be undertaken with no theological or other normative reasoning and must be subject to replication.

To make clear my motivations, my interest in the sociology of religion was based initially on my normative or theological interest in understanding variations in response to the Christian gospel. I believed God worked in and through human history and I wanted to see what explanations I could produce for these variations that would be empirically verifiable. I soon found that it was important to include examination of the spread of other religions besides Christianity, particularly Buddhism and Islam, which along with Christianity are the most widespread of all religions. It is an empirical fact, often not recognized by most scholars of religion, that these three religions have spread much more widely than any other religions. Thus, after choosing my topic for normative reasons, I pursued my study with a social scientific approach. This is perfectly acceptable in scientific studies.

Sociologists of religion are aware that they are considered as being in a marginal field within sociology. I suspect that one of the reasons may be that many social scientists see religion as so closely related to strong beliefs and emotions that religion cannot be studied objectively or without bias. Of course, they may well be biased against religion. However, the major founders of sociology, such as Emile Durkheim and Max Weber, as already noted, studied and wrote a great deal about religion. It was later in the twentieth century that sociologists began placing special emphasis on using mathematical or statistical methodologies and turned away from the study of religion. Although quantitative methods are very useful in studies of religion, good studies in religion and many other areas also often need to include personal interviews, historical comparative studies, textual analysis, or other qualitative methodologies. Thus, in spite of the bias against studies of religion by other sociologists, the fact that religion in its human side can be studied sociologically has remained and has even gained strength as social scientists have realized that religion is not fading away as many originally thought would happen as people became more rational.

It is true that the inner religious life, in particular the human capacity for faith and faith itself, is not directly observable and is largely ineffable. However, although religion centers on the intangible and ineffable, religions have always sought and created tangible representations of what they believe. In addition, it may be said that religious faiths (and nonfaiths) are preceded and followed by a very observable process that may be called the process of faith or nonfaith. The major parts of this process may be summarized as consisting of (1) historic persons and events, (2) social groupings from tribes, nations, religious groups or communities, clans, and families, (3) communication in spoken and written words, and (4) the mixture of laws, customs, values, attitudes, and movements that make up sociocultural forces. Christian theology itself speaks of the "marks of the church" based on Acts 2:42—the preaching of the word, the sacraments, fellowship or common disciplined life, and prayers. Note that these marks are largely observable and can be included in any study of the human side of Christianity.

I undertook my studies on why religions spread, looking primarily at Buddhism, Christianity, and Islam, by initially considering secular social factors that either blocked or facilitated their spread, but later adding essential religious content factors.[9] As previouly mentioned, a leading sociologist of religion, Rodney Stark, had drawn my attention to the fact that the content of religions, namely their beliefs and practices, could have a definite influence on their spread.[10] I had believed this, but had not expected a sociologist to emphasize this. While beliefs themselves are nonobservable, their expressions and practices are obviously observable. Furthermore, these beliefs and practices, contrary to the thought of many sociologists, can be studied as independent variables, namely as causes, not simply dependent variables or as effects of nonreligious causes.

It now remains for me to argue for the special value of the secular methodology of the social sciences, especially as applied to the study of religion. A secular approach may be used in almost all spheres of knowledge, but my specific point in this last section of the chapter is to argue that the secular methodology of science can function as a protection from false and even harmful human ideas that may be introduced by religious or other normative perspectives. Throughout history up to the present there have been many ideas about the natural world, including natural human life, that have been wrong or harmful. This includes many ideas held by religious people, for example, that the world is flat or that the sun circled the earth. These errors are obvious and noncontroversial in the present, although they were controversial in the past. Most recently and especially igniting the so-called war between science and religion is the clinging of many religious people, especially biblical literalists, to views that are strongly opposed to evolution. In the meantime, the theory of evolution is highly useful in medical studies, not to speak of the study of animal and human history. The opposition of Christians to evolution has helped to fuel opposition by secularists to any faith or religion in general. In addition to opposing evolutionary theory, many Christians oppose scientific work on climate warming and gender studies. This is the latest fuel for secularism.

A recent issue of *National Geographic* described "The War on Science" as including opposition to climate change, evolution, the moon landing,

9. Montgomery, *Why Religions Spread*.
10. Stark, *One True God*.

vaccinations, and genetically modified food.[11] Because of attacks on some of these, some scientists may in turn attack religion, but most others, including Christian scientists, simply ignore both their religious and secular attackers unless they supply credible scientific evidence. True faith is immune from scientific or any other attack, but religious people have had, and still have, faulty ideas about the world which need correction. Unfortunately, wrong ideas may be clung to for long periods of time and become a basis for harmful behavior. Some of the most damaging ideas, but also the most difficult to modify or correct, are the mistaken ideas of human behavior. The social sciences are particularly useful in explaining the sources of prejudice, discrimination, authoritarianism, rejection of change, and a variety of other values and motivations that may be based in socioeconomic class, ethnicity, race, and gender in addition to socialization and sociocultural context. These subjectively based and usually unconscious attitudes and opinions are extremely difficult to study and therefore make the social sciences controversial both among social scientists and the general public. Nevertheless, patient and careful study can contribute to bringing changes in attitudes and behaviors. It takes humility for those who claim to be following the revelation of God to accept examination by social scientists, but such examination can yield the fruit of spiritual growth and social progress.

Up to now I have not emphasized the limitations of a secular scientific perspective and methodology. Clearly only a theological or philosophical approach can set forth beliefs about God and realities that are beyond the natural world. As noted, these approaches are more comprehensive than a secular scientific one, or any other approach that is secular. Furthermore, religion can inspire and motivate people in a way that is beyond the power of science. The secular has a special weakness in not being able to enable people to find ultimate meaning and purpose in life. It is also not well equipped in the area of mutual relationships among people or in building community that is based on trust and forgiveness. Nevertheless, the secular should be considered a gift from God as a corrective discipline in tandem with the natural world, but like all gifts it is subject to misuse, the greatest one being when it is universalized and in effect, deified. In the meantime, people of faith have a responsibility to protect the secular and to make the best use of it, which is primarily for adding to knowledge that corrects old knowledge. Scientists have their biases, some of which may well

---

11. Achenbach, "The Age of Disbelief," 34–47.

be anti-religious, but the value of the scientific method is that it is able to expose biases, including those of scientists, although sometimes only over time.

I believed that the right use of the secular scientific approach in sociology of religion could be very helpful in clarifying what happened before my eyes—a Christian movement among the aboriginal people in Taiwan—without falling back on the religious answer that it was simply the work of God's Spirit. It certainly was that, but this begs the question: What religious and secular forces did God use? Yes, there were important religious content factors, but there were also important nonreligious factors (which I believe God used) that were important for facilitating or blocking the spread of Christianity, as well as of other religions. One of the greatest factors being the quality of intersocietal relationships, particularly domination of one society over another. (The responsiveness of Korea to the gospel being a good example since it was one of the few Asian countries not dominated by a Western country, but by its neighbor Japan)

As I remained in touch with the sociology of religion community, I noticed that there were a number of other areas of religious or church life that were helpfully researched. Some of these areas were congregational life, church professionals, youth religious and nonreligious life, gender and religion, religious change, and globalization and religion. Although denominational research offices participated and sometimes led meetings of sociologists of religion, one of my disappointments was that my mainline church seminaries were generally not well represented at the sociology of religion meetings.

Conclusion

The secular methodology of science is very well established, especially in the natural sciences. It has proven its great value in bringing increased understanding of the natural world and making possible many technologies that have greatly benefitted human life. The social sciences, because of the difficulty of examining human behavior, advanced more slowly than the natural sciences. Although well established in academia, the value of the social sciences is not as well established in the public mind as the natural sciences. The subfield of sociology of religion, in which I specialized, perhaps faces the most difficult struggle to find acceptance. This is because although religion has many outward manifestations, it involves the inner life, which is the most difficult aspect of human life to examine. Thus, most social scientific theories of religion require considerable elaboration and may be entirely replaced or redirected. The theory of the decline of religions in the process of secularization is one of these.

There is a strong community of scholars in the sociology of religion with three major professional associations in the United States: one originating in the Roman Catholic Church, a second originating among Protestants, and the third originating primarily from academia. However, now the three associations have overlapping memberships and are completely nonsectarian. In addition, there is an international society dedicated to the social scientific study of religion, as are numerous other associations in nations around the world. I have found people of faith, no faith, and anti-faith in all of the associations to which I belong. I have also found ongoing tensions and conflicts within the field that seem to revolve around how to deal with the inner capacity, or source(s), of faith, which is essentially nonempirical and even ineffable. In spite of the problems of acceptance and the internal struggles, the social scientific studies of religion will continue to contribute to the self-understanding of religious groups.

As a personal note, I must add that after years of reading primarily social scientific and historical books and articles, I found so many of my friends reading primarily novels or, if not fiction, then reading nonfiction accounts by journalists and people, often with experience in government, with stories to tell of their experiences in various parts of the world and their opinions about national policies. This experience emphasized for me that people really live by their opinions, including myself. I also came to realize that many fiction and nonfiction writers could give accounts that touched in some way—whether realistically or not—the inner personal life of people and the sense of the social context of events in ways that social scientists could not. This has reinforced my belief in the complementarity of all true knowledge. At the same time, I see glimpses of hope for the future influence of sociology of religion as it influences some religious thinkers and teachers by its uncovering various influences in the areas of faith, especially the faith of youth, and of vital religious organized life, including how the life of faith is spread—the area that especially interests me.

CHAPTER 5

Secular Methodology in Government

ALTHOUGH SCIENCE HAS SUPPORTIVE norms and a normative ethos, scientists rather clearly recognize scientific theorizing does not attribute causal factors to God. They even do not have to recognize the supportive norms for the early natural philosophers of a rational, not arbitrary, God who created a world with patterns to be rationally discovered. They also do not have to recognize openly the normative ethos of current science identified by Merton.[1] Scientists in their work only need to proceed with the secular methodology of science.

In contrast, governments are more likely to espouse overt supportive norms in the form of an ideology or a religion itself. In fact, governments and the societies they lead or dominate, unlike science, need an ideology that can be the basis for a common civil creed or a social contract. Politicians recognize that people in a nation or society need the unifying force of a basic agreement on certain beliefs and values. This helps to explain the historic alliance between governments and religions. Rulers seek legitimacy from religious sources and religions are glad to provide legitimacy from God in exchange for a religious monopoly protected by the government.

This age-old story was formally changed by the United States, although the roots of this change were in Europe. As far as I am concerned, this is the exceptionalism of the United States, not any kind of inherent superiority of its people. Every nation has its unique and valuable characteristics, and, I would add, physical beauty. However, two traditional alliances of governments were broken in the United States: the alliance of the nation with one ethnicity and with one religion. Before the Unites States, nations developed naturally with one dominant ethnic group. The Christian gospel spread to the European tribes, which largely represented ethnic groups, after which

1. See ch. 1, pp. 3–4.

they each eventually developed nation-states and a nationalistic spirit. Thus most nations are united by ethnic similarity. Although a positive result was the growth of self-respect and national accomplishments, the evil result was the constant warfare that developed between the nations. At the same time, the European nations continued the age-old alliance of governments and a religion in order to give legitimacy to governments and a monopoly position to the unifying religion, thus aiding religions to follow ethnic lines. At first, the various European ethnicities and religions were mixed in the United States, but then, over a long period of time and with a difficult struggle (including the Civil War and much conflict over civil rights) extending all the way up to the present time, various non-European ethnicities and non-Western religions became part of the ethnic and religious diversity of the nation. Supporting this diversity was that from the beginning no one religion was designated as official. Although the foundation of the nation has religious roots, its government *operation* became specifically secular. Some Euro-Americans resist recognizing the secularity of the government and that principles and ideals, rather than ethnicity, have increasingly become the basis of the nation. The meritocracy of the military has helped, but the call of Martin Luther King, Jr. for the nation to live up to its ideals, followed by his martyrdom (like Abraham Lincoln's), has set a standard for the nation to base itself in universal human principles of democracy with freedom and protection of human rights.

Thus, the background to the establishment of a secular government included certain geopolitical events seen in the struggle against persecution by European governments through their official religions, but also the migration (including forced migration of slaves) of religiously and ethnically diverse peoples to the New World. Before the forming of the United States, the questioning of the established religious authority by the Protestant Reformation had broken the long alliance of the established Roman Catholic Church with governments that had existed since the fourth century. Not surprisingly, this alliance followed the age-old and prevailing pattern in the world of the relationship of governments and religions. However, in addition to opening the door to the secularization of knowledge—which had been dominated by the church—that accompanied the religious revolt, the Reformation also opened the door to the secularization of governments imbued with the spirit of nationalism. It is this spirit that had made the Protestant Reformation successful, at least in northern Europe. The secularization of governments proceeded slowly because of the traditional relationship of governments to religion, but probably also because of the continuing recognition of the felt need for a unifying religious basis for societies. Secular ideologies for governments were to come later, beginning with the French Revolution (which later backtracked) and eventually producing fascism (which coopted religion), and Communism (which tried to eliminate religion) in the twentieth century.

The countries that accepted Protestantism, in large part made possible because of the rise of nationalism, maintained alliances with a dominant church. Even France, with the later anti-religious emphasis of the French Revolution, returned to a recognition of the special favored status of the Roman Catholic Church. Now, even after the atheistic Communist movement initially succeeded in Russia, almost all the countries that came under Communist governments (including the Soviet Union itself), at least in the West, have returned to favoring the traditional or mother churches in their lands. The pattern of the close relationship of European governments to dominant or monopolistic religions stands in contrast to the United States, which was largely populated by religiously and ethnically diverse sets of immigrants. Although churches lost a great deal of influence in European societies, they maintained a formal relationship to governments. In the United States, the opposite took place: the formal relationship of churches to the government was lost, but religions remained vital and gained a great deal of influence in society. Isn't there a lesson here for religions to follow a road of humility regarding power?

In the United States, the broad religious foundations of the nation are expressed in the Declaration of Independence, which states, "all men are created equal and endowed by their Creator with certain unalienable rights." While this is not a secular, but a religious foundation, the principle of equality is easily agreed to by all people, including nonbelievers. Human equality and human rights were also proclaimed in the French Revolution so that secular lovers of the Enlightenment can claim them as secular values. Nevertheless, it is arguable that human equality, and the rights that go with it, are ineffable and actually firmly based in divine creation. In other words, human beings are demonstrably not equal, but only equal in the sight of God, from whom they also receive a certain dignity. At any rate, though these ideals are the normative foundation of secular democracies, they are also the basis for continued challenges for democracies to live up to their ideals, which was the specific challenge issued by the religious and social leader, Martin Luther King, Jr.

In addition to having normative foundations, as in science, the secular method of government in secular democracies continually has to face moral issues related to government policies and programs. We remember that all human beings have moral sensibilities and they come into play in how governments are organized. This is certainly true in the United States, where the population is very religious and many people are committed to their moral views and ideals. Their moral views are often given a religious origin by these believing people. However, in spite of the strong moral arguments people use to move political action, the actual governmental decisions are never couched in religious terms. In other words, God cannot be used to support legislative actions or judicial decisions, at least in their writing. This is why the United States can be called a secular democracy. The Constitution of the United States does not mention God and it is never permitted to call upon a particular religious doctrine to justify governmental action. This would be breaking the First Amendment of the Constitution, which forbids making a law establishing a religion or a religious set of beliefs. If this were to happen, people with no religion and religious people who do not believe in the particular doctrine used to support an action would both claim that the government was acting against the Constitution.

One of the best examples of the secular nature of the United States government is in relation to laws related to abortion. Some people believe that human life begins at conception, meaning an embryo should be treated as a human being. This belief is a religious belief, but no laws can be made using God's will or revelation as justification or rationalization for abortion laws. Some religious people do not believe that human life begins at conception, but that *potential* human life begins at conception and gains potentiality as long as it lives within the mother. Thus, with these different religious views in the population, a law cannot be couched in religious terms without denying the beliefs of some. Of course, the government in the First Amendment is also not allowed to prohibit the free exercise of religion. As we know from history, the two-part prohibition of the Constitution (against establishment of religion and against prohibiting the free exercise of religion) has been the basis of numerous arguments in the courts. Nevertheless, in spite of all the religious convictions that motivate and inspire people, as in science, the operation of the government is secular. Politicians may speak and act out of religious motives, explaining their actions as based on their religious faith. Many voters like to hear that those they elect have religious faith, at least the one or ones that accord with their beliefs, usually a version of Christianity or at least more broadly a faith in God, but in the actual rationale for legislation and government programs, a religious rationale is not allowed. The secular method in government is a protection from unwanted religious ideas backed by religious authorities. The founding fathers in the United States felt the need for this type of protection based on what they had experienced (some of it in colonial days) or heard about in Europe. As a result, they also established a democratic type of government that would prevent the rise and domination of both a religious and a secular, nondemocratic government, like the ones which arose in Europe on the basis of an anti-religious ideology.

As Martin Luther King, Jr. did, Americans can appeal to ideals and morals without mentioning God. Interestingly, in America there is a rather strong suspicion of religiosity and piousness that appears in its literature and drama, as well as in ordinary conversation. The legal prohibition of alcohol became a clear example to the American people of the danger of legislation in which the morals of some are imposed on others. I should add a very important point about morality, and that is that the moral positions of Christians have been very questionable for many people, such as support of slavery and racial segregation, Christian condemnation of women's and LGBT rights, and Christian support of ultranationalism and opposition to the United Nations. Neglect of the environment and many Christians holding an anti-science view have also been harmful. Some secularists appear to have higher moral views to some Christians than the views of their fellow Christians.

As noted, the nations of Europe were built on ethnic groups that tended to adopt a single type of Christianity. This tended to keep the formal tie between the governments and the majority religion, even though the governments moved in a secular direction. It took a dramatic geographic shift of diverse European populations coming to the New World (an accident of history or providential, depending on your point of view) to create an unprecedented situation—ethnically and religiously diverse people seeking to establish a new and unified nation. This is an example of how I and other Christians believe God works in history without making it scientifically provable that it is God's hand. Another major example of what Christians might interpret as God working in history is the influence of geopolitical events on the collapse of Western colonialism after World War II. This was followed by the great growth of Christianity in Africa and China, as well as openness in other areas of the world. The spread of secularization itself may be seen as a positive development for the spread of the gospel because of its contribution to religious freedom and the clarification of religious choices.

In one sense it could be said that religion, specifically Christianity, was humbled by the action of the United States to keep organized religion out of the government. There were many memories of oppressive regimes in Europe that were backed by official Christian bodies. Special favors were also given to the favored Christian denominations in Europe. Even in the United States, Congregationalists were favored in New England until as late as 1831, when the official relationship was disolved in Massachusetts. The Anglicans were favored in New York and Virginia until the new national Constitution was established, but challenges from other Christian groups, such as Baptists and Presbyterians, had begun in colonial times. The leaders of the nation had enough of the flavor of the Old World arrangements to know that they did not want a continuation of what they or their forebears had suffered in Europe. Even though most of the founders were either religious people or at least not anti-religious, they agreed that government decisions should be made for common sense or practical, namely secular, reasons. Because of the many opportunities for religious bodies to expand freely, there was little sense that they were disadvantaged by not having political power in the government. Actually, relief from political responsibility gave religious leaders more time to carry out religious work, whether it was evangelistic or social service, which could include influencing government programs. Furthermore, as the nineteenth century proceeded, many new churches, mission movements, and religious societies were organized. Because of the great spaces in America and the isolation of small communities, people placed a great emphasis on individual initiative and on local organization. A problematic development was the wide ownership of guns, which was considered acceptable, but the National Rifle Association under new leadership in the 1970s began raising fears that guns would be taken away. This created an obsession for many over the Second Amendment and gun ownership. The open spaces and many opportunities for self-supporting work also supported individualism, localism, and a certain antipathy to central governments in both state and church.

America inherited the tradition, already seen in Europe, of questioning religious pretensions and religious hierarchy. People felt that religious people, just because they were religious and used religious words, could not necessarily be trusted with the use of power, including in the church. In literature and in common culture, people gave full expression to biblical themes that were critical of hypocrisy and religious pretension. This tended to reinforce the value of keeping religious leaders and their organizations out of positions of political power. Religious leaders needed to be able to prove themselves as religious leaders in their own churches by being able to attract followers primarily by their effective preaching, but also through their leadership in bringing about spiritual and social transformation. Therebfore, the nature of religious power became distinguished from political power. In this way, secular government proved to be beneficial—not harmful—to religions.

One of the major results of the disestablishment of religion in America was the creation of a vibrant civil society. Churches founded numerous educational institutions, hospitals, welfare agencies, and a variety of organizations to promote various social and political causes. Many organizations initiated by churches (including educational institutions, as we shall see) were spun off and became independent of any specific church. In addition to the movements within the churches to win followers to Christ called the Great Awakenings, a number of social movements were initiated, not necessarily by churches, but often by Christians and like-minded people who impacted society, like the Abolitionist Movement, the Women's Movement, and later the Civil Rights Movement. The Labor Union Movement—more secular than others—did have an impact on society, but it took until some decades into the twentieth century and has since waned in its influence. However, it was, and is, supported by followers of the Christian social gospel and to some extent merged with the Civil Rights Movement. The amendment prohibiting the sale of alcohol was repealed, but there remain many restrictions on liquor at the local level. Gun control remains an important moral issue with religious and nonreligious people on both sides of the issue. Volunteerism became a hallmark of American civil society. The point of this paragraph is that the limitation of government involvement in religion actually helped to create a civil society in which people of many different viewpoints—including religious people and organizations—could have an impact on government and society in general. Religion and many other causes had to rest on the power of persuasion and also the political action of individuals and organizations (including churches) rather than the power of government.

An important qualification needs to be made. With the reduction both of religious power in government and of political power over religion with secularization, the rise of economic and business power may be seen in

Western societies. Capitalism became the major economic system of Western societies. The eighteenth- and nineteenth-century Industrial Revolution greatly accelerated the ability of people to acquire wealth, sometimes very great wealth. In many respects, the power of religious bodies was replaced by the economic power of business and industrial entities. Skyscrapers replaced cathedrals as the highest buildings. The Marxist reaction to the excesses of the economically powerful did not succeed in gaining political power in Western Europe or the United States, but rather in traditional societies where economic and political power were closely wedded. In the West, capitalism evolved into a variety of regulated forms. However, the limitation of economic power by government policies took place over time through a series of reform movements because of the evident problems brought about by the lack of regulation. Both the benefits and the injuries caused by the capitalist free market led to the various systems of regulated capitalism in various nations. This took place basically because of the power of civil societies being combined with democratic governments to carry out reforms that brought some controls to corporate business power. Supporters and critics of economic power have become major players in civil society and in government. Religious groups and individuals are divided, but are able to inject moral (not religious) arguments into the public debates, but the terms of debate are basically secular when it comes to creating government policies. Furthermore, a widening gap in wealth in the United States and most of the world raises important questions about the misuse of economic power on the national level, but especially on the international level with globalization.

Conclusion

The secular government of the United States does not mean an anti-religious government. It means that it does not favor any one religion and does not hinder religious expression. It also means that governmental decisions are not justified by the government for religious reasons or because they are said to be approved by God. At the same time, religious people and religious groups may advocate for governmental programs and policies within civil society. The arguments for particular policies to finally be accepted must be on the basis of what is recognized as just, and what benefits people according to a majority of elected officials. Of course, special interests expressed through lobbyists have a great deal of influence that can either aid or inhibit good governmental actions. What reinforces the secular or nonreligious position of the government is that various religious people and church bodies have differed greatly among themselves on what is just and beneficial. In the many reform movements such as the Women's Movement, the Labor Movement, and the Civil Rights Movement there was both unity and division among religious groups in advancing liberty and justice for all. This illustrates the need for both religious advocacy and not giving political power to a particular religious group.

In the United States, religious argumentation as such is not necessarily considered relevant and may be challenged by those with other religious views, especially when they see religious views as harmful. In this way, living up to the principle of liberty and justice for all takes center stage as being the central duty of a secular government. A secular methodology in government has the effect of making morality, not religion as such, the central issue for governments. Conservatives may argue that same-sex marriage and homosexuality are forbidden by God, thus bringing religion and morality together, but others may argue that their religion does not make such behavior immoral. Instead, their religion calls for the right of two individuals, regardless of gender, to make a marriage commitment to each other. Thus, justice or right action by the government becomes the central purpose for secular governments, just as truth and authenticity become the central goal for secular science. However, just as religion is removed from government, so the government cannot make theological decisions. In the same way, secular science cannot make theological decisions. In this way, the secular in science and government becomes a protection for religion by keeping faulty religious thought out of knowledge about the world and faulty religious thought and action out of governmental policymaking. Paradoxically, the religious doctrine of human sin and fallibility became a foundation stone for the positive use of the secular in government, as well as in science.

CHAPTER 6

Secular Methodology in Education

THIS CHAPTER HAS BEEN the most difficult for me to write because although the place of secular methodology in education is very important, the limitations and dangers of the secular are especially revealed in the field of education. The secularization of schools of higher education that were founded by Christians has probably come under more criticism by some Christians than almost any other area of secularization.

The fact is that a majority of subjects in general education can be taught from a secular perspective. Furthermore, students need to learn secular methodologies (all part of the secular as methodology) because they are very useful and needed in today's world. But students also need to explore and learn about the meaning and purpose of life, and the secular by definition cannot teach these, at least at the ultimate level. Secular methodologies have helped create a high level of diversity in knowledge, skills, and living, so that unified meaning and purpose are hard to envision today with only secular methodology. Only the purpose of various specializations or professions can be envisioned, which is a highly limited view of life's goals. Starting with the secular methodology of science, we recognize that it has been used to accomplish wonderful things, like bringing better health and standards of living and uncovering many secrets of nature, for example. Because of these accomplishments, it is tempting for some, especially in academia, to virtually worship science even though it has no answers for many of life's deep questions. Unfortunately, some may simply adopt the secular mental construction in which no cause is attributed to God. They deal with God's creation simply on its own terms, but also as related only to themselves rather than to God.

Secular methodologies in the many scientific fields (both natural and social), and also in the humanities, clearly do not require religious reasoning, but I am emphasizing in this book that scholars and actors in all fields may be inspired and motivated by their faith and see their work as an offering to God because they see all reality as related to God. Obviously a choice has to be made. Clearly much education and study can be carried out without reference to God or religion, but if students are to do more than just acquire knowledge and skill in their education or only prepare for a career, they need to find meaning and purpose in life. Beyond knowledge and skill, education needs to transmit or enable students as they mature to discover how to think spiritually and morally. Thus students, especially at the higher-education level, need to be allowed to explore and think for themselves in order for their faith to be genuine.

I will state at the beginning that I believe a distinction should be made between Christian education and general education. Christian education is one of the primary responsibilities of the church because it pertains directly to faith. Actually, a better term is "Christian nurture" as used in the "Great Ends of the Church" in the Presbyterian Church (USA) *Book of Order*, because nurture implies a clearer spiritual purpose than simply education.[1] Education places the emphasis on knowledge rather than a spiritual relationship. General education must cover a wide array of subjects, most of which can be approached with secular methodologies. The state must take up general education, but Christians have historically initiated many schools of general education, recognizing that they can be of great benefit to people. What gives church-related schools a complex task, and makes this chapter difficult, is that a general education, if it seeks to educate the whole person, should point to the importance of gaining purpose and meaning in life and give students opportunities to discover these important values, or at least the best path toward their discovery. We must admit that religious thinking may be, and has been, mistaken and even harmful in notions about the natural world and human history, as well as in how to govern nations. Beyond that, theological ideas may be wrong. Secular methodology can contribute helpful corrections and improvements to all thinking and activity, including religious thinking and activity. However, the difficulty of secular methodology in education is that when it becomes dominant,

---

1. The second of the "Great Ends of the Church" of the Presbyterian Church (USA) is "shelter, nurture, and spiritual fellowship of the children of God." To mention the other "Great Ends of the Church," the first is "the proclamation of the gospel for the salvation of humankind." Following the second Great End we have: "the maintenance of divine worship, the preservation of the truth, the promotion of social righteousness, and the exhibition of the Kingdom of Heaven to the world."

as it has in much education, it damages a central element in good education, which is to enable students to find ultimate meaning and purpose for their lives and the larger world, and to think morally in addition to analytically in secular thinking.[2] With all the paradoxes involved with the use of secular methodology, its successes and its limits, it is not surprising that I, as well as churches and societies, should have to struggle to find the best place for secular methodology and religious/spiritual thinking in general education, a place that is presently being contested among Christians. This contestation stretches particularly across most Protestant denominations, causing some schools to break their connection to theologically conservative denominations and other schools to connect to more theologically conservative associations of schools and operate with little connection to a founding denomination or to operate simply as independent Christian or Christ-centered schools.

In approaching the contested approach for church- or Christian-founded schools to general education (I am not concerned in this chapter with state schools), I have been influenced by Mark R. Schwehn, who described the rise of the influence of the secular in education, the dangers it has introduced, and the important contribution of religion or the spiritual to education.[3] It is as though in general education that both the value of secular methodology and its limitations and dangers may be seen most clearly. I did not realize that I would encounter this fact, but it is somewhat understandable that education should be a difficult task because in education a society seeks to transmit to the young the most important things in life. In addition, young people are very impressionable and young adults are dealing with issues of their identities and directions for their future lives, such as work and marriage.

Schwehn speaks of the secular approach to knowledge as the "Weberian ethos" based on Max Weber's views expressed in "Academics as a Vocation."[4] Weber saw that the secular approach will virtually dominate the search for knowledge. This seems to have taken place in a large portion of general education, but I hope this is not the case in church-related schools. Of course, Weber was one of the most influential founders of

---

2. Secularists might challenge this and that is why I wrote "ultimate meaning." Nonbelievers in God might have much to say about purpose and meaning in the present life, as well as about morals.

3. Schwehn, *Exiles from Eden*, viii, 6–16.

4. Weber, "Science as a Vocation," 129–56. (Identical to "Academics as a Vocation.")

my secondary discipline of the social sciences.⁵ The Weberian ethos is especially strong in research universities, which have become a model for many schools. My post-theological graduate work, beginning when I was thirty-nine, was in social scientific studies of religion as I searched for answers to why people responded in different ways to religions which were introduced to them from the outside. This was in the irregular spread of Christianity that I saw in Taiwan and the rest of the world, and it became my central interest. I felt that the secular social scientific approach yielded some important answers to my question, even if it did not provide the complete answer. From the very beginning I realized the social scientific approach and the theological approach were in sharp contrast and I came to believe that it was important to distinguish them in my writing. I believed that the theological approach was more comprehensive and could—and should—incorporate secular methodology and theory, whereas secular methodology and theory could contribute to, but not incorporate, theological knowledge.⁶ On the basis of my secular studies, I could see important implications for the theological (missiological) understanding of successful and nonsuccessful mission work.

Let us go back to see how we got to where we are in the field of education. All societies have sought to transmit knowledge to subsequent generations, but this transmission was initially through the informal socialization of the young in order for them to learn skills and wisdom from those who lived before them. With the development of writing, a special few became scribes and education became more formalized, but was generally limited to a few, often future religious leaders. We know them as the religious specialists such as rabbis, priests, ministers, and imans. In China, education was more secular, except for important liturgy related to heaven or the Supreme Emperor, especially for government officials or literati. In Europe, which eventually became the leader in establishing advanced educational institutions, the church originally provided education primarily to the clergy, although initially only a few advanced very far. In the West, Latin was the most important language for literacy in the church, but in the Christian East, Greek was the scholarly language with translations of the Bible to Gothic and Slavic languages taking place, using the Greek alphabet.

5. Schwehn, *Exiles from Eden*, 6–16.

6. The distinction between the two approaches is reflected in my writing in which I use a sociological approach in the main part of my books, but include either an Appendix or a last chapter on the theological or missiological implications of the study. See my book *Why Religions Spread*.

Although translations of the Bible to European languages began (with opposition from the church), it was especially the printing of the Bible in small print and the creation of many school books in the nineteenth century that spurred the development of public education, so important today in many lands, particularly so that ordinary people could read the Bible. Many churches also served as schoolhouses or they built them, as in Scotland, where the literacy rate became even higher than in England. In America, churches or church members also built schoolhouses and also founded numerous colleges, some of which became present-day elite universities. Basically, literacy and education were viewed as being benefiicial to all people. In that spirit, in the nineteenth century, missionaries built schools and hospitals wherever they went around the world. This alone manifests a kind of parallel between education and health care. That is, they were considered a good thing so that all people, whatever their faith, race, or culture, could benefit from them. Unintentionally, this also demonstrated a basis for the secularization of both health care and education as people of all faiths and no faith could benefit by both education and modern medicine and also become proficient in both fields. In some countries, government-operated schools became more highly rated than church schools.

In the Middle Ages, the established churches (Roman Catholic and Orthodox) had overall authority and theology was the queen of sciences. However, as we noted in chapter 2, the Protestant Reformation's challenge to established religious authority over theological knowledge opened the possibilities for new approaches to all knowledge. An example was Francis Bacon's challenge to dominant Aristotelian thought in the early seventeenth century. As already noted, natural philosophers (scientists) became organized later in the century as they institutionalized the search for natural knowledge (creating the Royal Academy of England in 1660, and the Academie de Sciences of France in 1666). As science spread in the subsequent centuries, the usefulness of the secular methodology of science became increasingly recognized. The discoveries of science stimulated a great expansion in all fields of knowledge, using secular methodologies that proved so useful in science. The social sciences developed as the scientific method was applied to the study of human behavior, but in addition, secular methodologies of objective criticism were applied in history, philosophy, literature, and the rest of the humanities ("criticism" meaning "analysis," not simply criticism with a negative meaning).

SECULAR METHODOLOGY IN EDUCATION

In the United States, public education gradually became available to all people, but the issue of the secular in education contrasting with a faith approach became evident and has continued to the present. Regarding the overall process of secularization, Christian Smith and colleagues documented this process in the United States in education and other fields.[7] In the first part of the nineteenth century, the leaders in public education saw their responsibility as being to teach a general Christianity. However, the leaders of the Roman Catholic Church objected that the public schools were teaching Protestant Christianity. The Roman Catholic Church, as well as some other churches, established schools to teach their faith combined with general education. By the 1870s, the leaders in public education realized that they needed to secularize the approach in public education for a diverse society, and proceeded in this process well into the twentieth century. Even in 1882, Cincinnati stopped offering devotions in schools. It could be said that the last step in the long history of the secularization of public education was when prayer was eliminated from public schools in 1962.

At the same, but beginning even earlier, higher education began the secularization process. Churches or Christian groups established innumerable colleges and universities, some of the most famous being in the Northeast where Puritans had emphasized the life of the mind and an educated clergy. Many, if not most, of the colleges and universities established by churches and Christians across the country have increasingly become independent institutions, even though many have remained church-related. After much thought, my argument explaining the major influence in the secularization of education is not so much that it was the result of anti-religious attitudes (although they were present, especially in higher education), but that so much knowledge can be effectively taught from a secular perspective and with secular methods. Even religion itself can be taught with a secular methodology in which religions are described and also analyzed in terms of the influence of societies upon them and of their influence on societies (the latter being often neglected by scholars.)

Thus, I believe secularization in general education has been as much a natural process as a matter of the loss of religious faith. In other words, people have experienced the secular approach as useful for gaining many kinds of knowledge and skills. At the same time, many major institutions and their supporting churches recognized the need for education from a specifically religious or theological perspective and established theological

---

7. Smith, *Secular Revolution*.

schools. This highlights to me the distinction between a secular and a theological approach to knowledge. When seminaries were not established, most church-related schools taught religion in courses, provided chaplains for their students, and encouraged the formation of religious organizations on campuses. At the same time, these schools taught numerous courses in fields introducing secular methods and knowledge. Even religion and Bible courses introduced students to secular methods of study, mainly in biblical criticism and in church history. This is in contrast to the approach taken by churches themselves where efforts are made to advance and develop the faith of the believing community. In other words the approach is more clearly normative in theological schools and churches than in church-related schools established to appeal to the general public with a wide array of courses. The danger, as mentioned above, is that these church-related schools become dominated by the Weber ethos, and thus become mainly oriented toward training for jobs and careers, instead of helping students explore the meaning and purpose of their lives. Conservative Christians think that mainline church-related schools have allowed themselves to become too secularized. This should certainly be recognized as a danger and that is all the more reason why it would be wise for them to consider seriously the thought of Schwehn and also the efforts of the Lily Foundation (discussed below) to get church-related schools to help students consider the meaning and purpose of life through organized gatherings and retreats.

Before considering the options for mainline church-related colleges, let us consider the steps taken by the other party within Protestantism. The other party, currently having the label "evangelical," is more assertive in attaching expressions of the Christian faith to education. The history of modern evangelicalism was initially shaped by the dispensational-pre-millenarian or fundamentalist movement that developed very much in opposition to the mainline churches that began interpreting the Bible with secular methodologies, which are generally used in studying literature. These methodologies were introduced primarily from Germany beginning in the nineteenth century. Fundamentalists reacted strongly in the opposite direction and asserted that the Bible was inerrant and largely to be interpreted literally. This modernist-fundamentalist controversy came to a head in the 1920s, which centered on the view and interpretation of the Bible, and led in the 1930s and 1940s to the basic division in American Protestantism of mainline and evangelical churches. Some conservative Christians, who were more educated than other conservatives, adopted the term "evangelical" in contrast to "fundamentalist" as a term without the connotation of judgmental and militant attitudes, but rather emphasizing the proclamation of the gospel. Whatever variations there may be in telling the story of the division between the mainline and evangelical churches and Christians, the two groups have developed broadly different approaches to education in colleges and universities and broadly different cultures within their churches.

Fundamentalists established many Bible institutes, usually teaching dispensationalism, many of which later became colleges and universities. Probably the best term for most of these schools today is evangelical or conservative Christian. The present situation is best illustrated by the Council of Christian Colleges and Universities (CCCU), which represents "Christ-centered" evangelical schools. They generally consider mainline-related schools as not sufficiently Christian or as even being non-Christian and dominated by secular humanism. Because of the explicit statements of faith in the form of a confession of faith that includes a statement of the authority of the Bible, as well as other statements of faith associated with conservative Christianity, the Christ-centered schools, in my view, in effect make themselves into ecclesiastical bodies. I believe this becomes a limiting factor in teaching all the subjects needed in higher education that are not specifically religious. This also limits the ability to teach a wide range of students and tends to limit the exploration of the great variety of thinking in various religions. Although often quite distinct from Christianity, other religions can have viewpoints and practices which Christians may find helpful or which helps them appreciate their own faith traditions more fully.

However, I believe there is a deeper problem, which is a theological problem with practical effects. This reflects my mainline church perspective. "Christ-centered" is basically a theological term, which is best not used as a label. It is the central personal goal of Christians, but Christ-centered refers especially to the inner life of faith, and use of the term encourages the temptation to make judgments about the degree of Christ-centeredness of other individuals or organizations, and a search for what the signs of its presence or absence might be. Whether one is Christ-centered is a worthy question to ask oneself since no one is completely Christ-centered, but when the question is applied to others it does not encourage Christian unity or cooperation, but rather mutual judgment and condemnation. The fact is that unlike churches, schools need to teach many secular subjects and contribute to secular knowledge, as well as allow students to explore many fields of knowledge. This is not the task of the church. I believe it is best then for church- or Christian-founded schools to live with the simple designation of being church-related or of having a Christian heritage. That tradition in itself is an important witness to the Christian concern for the welfare of all peoples as aided by education that has proven to be a great help in raising standards of living.

My own view, obviously favoring the mainline church approach to education, is that it is not best for schools, particularly schools of higher education, to carry the name of Christian or especially of being Christ-centered. After saying this, I believe mainline church-related colleges and universities should learn lessons from conservative Christian schools and should seek in various ways to avoid being dominated by a secular perspective that does not consider spiritual and religious thought important. Beyond that, church-related colleges should continually examine themselves to consider how well they may be contributing to the journey of faith of students, both the opportunity to begin that journey and to progress on it. This could be considered nurturing, as in the Great Ends of the Church.

There needs to be an openness to hearing all expressions of faith, but a church-related school should certainly enable its students to hear the gospel of Jesus Christ, remembering that the nature of faith means that it cannot be imposed. However, basic faith development itself is left primarily to churches or religiously organized groups, including those on campus. In short, a low-key approach is taken to presenting the Christian faith in a manner which emphasizes individual responsibility to explore the meaning and purpose of life, leading to or enhancing a personal commitment to Jesus Christ while also entering into fellowship with other Christians. To me this indicates a confidence in the great appeal of Jesus Christ to all human beings, especially when Christians are not hindering the way of envisioning and perceiving Christ. I believe church-related schools need to continually examine how well this difficult task of clarifying the human vision of Christ is being done. I call this sharing the treasure that Christians have in Christ, which is the mission calling.

Recognizing the trend toward secularization in church-related schools, the Lily Foundation funded a $225-million, eight-year initiative on eighty-eight campuses that

> invited church affiliated colleges and universities to develop programing that would foster campus conversations about questions

of meaning and purpose, and in particular their religious underpinnings, which is the theology of vocation.[8]

They were offered $50,000 each for planning and for implementing the program. One would have to say that the Lily Foundation offer came from people who were concerned with the influence of the Weber ethos on church-related college campuses. Tim Clydesdale carried out a careful evaluation of the results of this initiative that included many interviews with participants. The planning of the "purpose exploration programs" was consistent with mainline church-related colleges in using an open inquiry that welcomed many points of view, including different faith perspectives. At the same time, Christian perspectives were certainly included as long as people listened respectfully to others. The focus of the gatherings was on vocation or meaning and purpose in life. Clydesdale joins a number of other scholars of American education in valuing "engaging spirituality on campus," but goes further to identify

> theologically embedded exploration of purpose and vocation that is especially generative among campus populations, and describing the broad impact that occurs when a critical mass of students and educators coalesces into a pro-exploration, self-containing community."[9]

I see the approach to learning in an open community as marking the major difference in the approach of the two main branches of Protestantism (mainline and evangelical) to education in their schools. In a word, mainline church-related schools seek to have communities of inquiry which are more open to a variety of ways of thinking so that there can be free inquiry and free choice in spiritual matters, which is considered to be consistent with being an educational institution. On the other hand, evangelical schools seek to define their school communities as clearly Christian, calling them "Christ-centered," which, although this might be denied by these schools, tends to set up barriers to free inquiry and open discussion and learning in the various secular fields of knowledge. In the long run, this will negatively affect educational standing. These schools may consider this the cost of being "Christ-centered," whereas others may consider that the Christian witness can maintain itself in a free environment. In other words, God is the author of all truth, and faith does not need to fear truth that is

---

8. Clydesdale, *Purposeful Graduate*, 2, 3.
9. Ibid., 212.

honestly gained. Excellence in education is a worthy goal of church-related schools. At the same time, a distinction exists between the approach of the mainline church-related colleges and mainline churches. Churches take on Christian education, or nurture specifically, whereas colleges seek to maintain an open community of inquiry for all students seeking both a general education and the purpose and meaning of life.

I am obviously biased toward the mainline church-related college approach, but admit that such schools might fall into an overly secularized approach that does not educate the whole person and leaves out the important spiritual aspect of life. (The purpose of the Lily Foundation funding was to encourage the creation of school communities that educate the whole person.) Improvements in church-related schools are always needed and some things may be learned from conservative schools' approaches. At the very least, I believe that the mainline church-related schools should make sure that the gospel of Jesus Christ is heard by students, meaning that the meaning and purpose of life that comes through faith in Jesus Christ is heard in the open inquiry in the educational community. I believe the church-related college, although not a church or a religious organization, should be no less than a free and open society in which the church is an active part and students have the opportunity to hear the gospel of Christ and learn to live a life of service to God's kingdom.

From my perspective, the difference in the two approaches is based on the different nature of secular knowledge and knowledge based on faith. The latter incorporates the former, but only after taking it seriously. Secular methodologies of study may actually contribute to faith knowledge and also may protect faith knowledge from errors. The knowledge based on faith ultimately belongs to, or arises from, the spirit or inner sensibilities. It is the kind of knowledge referred to in Isaiah 1:1, which says, "The ox knows it owner, and the donkey its master's crib; but Israel does not know, my people do not understand." There are outward expressions of this faith expressed inadequately in the various languages of the world in confessions of faith or creeds which Christian bodies have developed to guide the search for this real inner faith. The words of the confessions or creeds come from interpretations of the Bible understood as being in words that express divinely inspired faith responding to the self-revelation of God. The words that state beliefs may be studied and described by anybody in a secular manner. However, the same divine inspiration from the Holy Spirit that inspired the Bible is necessary to have the faith originally expressed in the

Bible. In other words, the words of the Bible and the statements of faith can be learned, expressed, and at least partially interpreted with a secular methodology. However, I believe the Holy Spirit is necessary for a fully adequate interpretation.

I believe Schwehn deals with the distinctive approach of church-related colleges in his discussion of the quest for community, knowledge as power, and education in a disordered world.[10] My interpretation and application of what Schwehn says is that God made human beings for community and this can be seen in how humans have evolved and what they seek, but also in mutual love and forgiveness that is imperfectly created by faith communities. Knowledge brings power and power can destroy community. This destruction can be encountered in educational institutions. These institutions need to recognize this danger and take steps to mitigate this destruction and find a path toward community. Finally, we live in a disordered world in which we cannot return to Eden (the realm from which all academics like Schwehn are exiles), but a church-related school should be honest in recognizing that secular knowledge, apart from being useful, can also be destructive when it becomes ideological (secularism). The church-related school should move forward in seeking the spiritual knowledge that gives purpose and meaning to life.

For understanding the place of spiritual or theological knowledge in education, it is useful to compare a theological seminary to a church-related college. A theological seminary or a specifically religious school is not simply an academic institution that must advance secular knowledge, but rather one that seeks to deepen understanding of theology and the Bible—not simply deepen understanding, but deepen faith itself. However, this may be aided by advancing secular knowledge of the Bible and theology through teachers who can teach in a way that conveys faith. In addition to being an educational institution, the theological institution is a worshipping community. It is attended by those who are either following a sense of a call from God to special service in the church or some other direct service to God. It is possible students are seeking to find out if service in the church is a possible calling for them, but at the least they want to live a life of service to God and human beings. Some students in colleges and universities might be on the same kind of quest, which might or might not send them on to theological school. This kind of spiritual knowledge of a calling is directly related to finding the meaning and purpose of life,

---

10. Ibid., 127–38.

although finding them certainly does not necessarily lead to a calling to serve God in the church. In either case, students need to find the meaning and purpose of life through personal spiritual experience. It is important that a church-related college employ one or more teachers or chaplains trained in a theological school, usually of the denomination with which college is related, to serve as a guide in the search for the deeper or ultimate meaning and purpose of life.

The Bible contains the sacred literature of the Jewish and Christian religions in the form of the Hebrew Scriptures for Jews and in the form of these same Scriptures plus the Greek New Testament for Christians. On the one hand, in theological schools and colleges, these Scriptures need to be studied like the Scriptures of any religion as human literature with the secular tools of literary and historical criticism. On the other hand, people of faith also believe they are the revelation of God to which they respond with faith. They include important elements of intellectual knowledge, but at their base they point to the reality of an encompassing and deep spiritual reality to which we relate through a faith. Ultimately, the meaning and purpose of life depends on such faith. However, there are many steps along the way so that faith is really a journey, a journey that never ends and a journey with many points of maturation through ongoing repentance combined with new faith. Formal education can only provide a way station on the journey of faith, but it needs to be at least that.

The usefulness and wide applicability of the secular approach to knowledge, and at the same time its limitation in being able to deal adequately with the deep human need for meaning and purpose, is the source of the struggle with the secular in education. Complicating the struggle is that there are less-than-ultimate meanings and secondary purposes for life that can be learned through secular methods. Further complicating the issue is the fact that faith-based reasoning has often been faulty and harmful and at the same time secular reasoning can make helpful contributions to faith-based reasoning. Because of these facts, I believe Christians in higher education, as well as theological education, should not isolate themselves from either secular studies or thinking from other religions.

Mainline churches founded many colleges and universities, which remain the main type of church-related schools, the term I prefer. These schools must teach many courses that are secular and open to all people, many of whom may not be Christian, especially if the school was established overseas. But if the church-related status is maintained, it should be possible, especially if it is in a Christian majority society like the United States, to offer courses in which the Christian gospel is offered, certainly not imposed. Of course, a Christian theological school is specifically a Christian school and offers a Christian education, as do Christian churches. Churches operate theological schools and education in their churches for their members and those who are interested in advancing the faith. It is worth noting that at least two Ivy League schools have theological seminaries attached to them. These are Harvard and Yale. The University of Dubuque is the only Presbyterian USA university with an affiliated theological seminary. Duke, Emory, Vanderbilt, and SMU are four large Methodist universities with theological schools, while Wake Forest and Mercer University are Baptist schools with seminaries. The generally small Presbyterian USA colleges and universities and other church-related schools have religion departments. In mainline church-related schools, teachers, usually trained in theological schools of the denomination, teach courses on the Bible and religion. What they teach—as well as what is taught in secular universities—may be a shock to students who have never heard of the human side of the Bible. It is understood by most mainline theologians that secular approaches to understanding the Bible do not destroy the faith, but actually provides a stronger and clearer foundation for it by aiding in understanding the Bible and the church in the world. However, this takes skill in teaching both faith and understanding. I would not recommend church-related schools offer courses in the Bible and Christianity which are taught by non-Christians, although other world religions may be taught by non-Christians. Church-related schools, as opposed to Christ-centered schools, usually teach the theological basis of the Christian faith and Christian history, not in an aggressive manner, but in a manner that emphasizes a thoughtful, critical, and exploratory approach by the students, who may be struggling with questions of faith and who need to know some of the failures of the church.

As already stated, the perspective of this book is that the secular is not anti-Christian or anti-religious *per se*, but rather provides a useful method for understanding and dealing with the world and human life, which includes religions. All people carry biases and can use data and information from the secular world in a way that is harmful and opposed to faith in God. However, scholars can use the same data or additional data and information in a secular approach to discount or offset the harm caused by those, including religious people, who misuse secular knowledge. My view in this book is that knowledge gained from the secular world, gained as objectively as possible, can be used to benefit humanity and can offset knowledge that is used to harm others. In other words, a nonbeliever does not have an advantage in using information from the secular world, but rather because the natural world is God's creation, the truth gained from it by secular methodology can have a very positive value for human life.

I believe the secular as a methodology is not inherently anti-religious, although I admit that taking the Bible and public prayer (not God) out of public schools and out of public life as a way of not favoring any particular religion tended to create a secular atmosphere. However, the possibility of expressing personal faith in a nonaggressive way is usually still possible. In the end, the secular atmosphere of public schools and the public sphere places a greater responsibility for Christian education on churches and Christian families. Those who choose to be anti-religious may and do use a secular methodology to advance their secularism, but when they are doing so they are injecting their personal opinions into a methodology that should be opinion-free. It is not the secular *per se*, but the worship of the secular—as in secularism or the universalizing of the secular—that becomes anti-Christian and anti-religious. Since self-criticism is an important element among thoughtful Christians, anti-Christians should be heard in a free society, but also there should be opportunities to answer criticisms. The issue is complex and it is not surprising that people of faith have taken different roads in dealing with the secular in education, which has led to different ways of opposing secularism as a philosophy or a substitute religion as discussed above.

My attitude toward extra ecclesiastical organizations (like colleges) founded by Christians was influenced by my experience working for the Federation of Protestant Welfare Agencies (FPWA) in New York City for seven years as a Liaison to Churches. It is an umbrella organization in the city for a set of welfare agencies, most of which were established by Protestant churches. It stands alongside two other large organizations—Catholic Charities and Jewish Philanthropies—which relate to their respective religious communities. The FPWA was declared "nonsectarian," but it sought especially to help churches in their service to their communities (this was my job as the Liaison to Churches.) One of the important discoveries I made was that churches and Christian organizations had founded and continued to found many agencies that were benefiting society. They are agencies serving the needs of children and the aging, sheltering the homeless, feeding programs, literacy programs, legal aid societies, and community organizations that carried out numerous programs which benefit communities. However, after their founding, many if not most of these agencies and programs were spun off to become independent nonprofit bodies with independent boards. In other words, they were secularized. Then there were the many hospitals with the names of religious bodies attached to them, but which were now operating independently of those bodies. I came to the conclusion that schools and many spun-off organizations were somewhat analogous to hospitals and have followed the same path as modern medicine, namely to become a way of service to all people. After all, most of the knowledge schools seek to convey can be studied with a secular approach, just as medicine can be practiced with secular knowledge and skills. However, we Christians believe that Christians can bring a special flavor or aroma to their medical or any other secular work. They thereby cease to be secular and become sacred tasks.

My suggestion is that in establishing and managing church-related schools it is useful to recognize a distinction between a secular approach to knowledge that only presents knowledge known through natural means and a theological or spiritual approach that recognizes a reality that is beyond the natural world. This difference should be made clear to students. It is even more important to recognize that there is a difference between knowledge about faith, which can be presented in a descriptive or secular manner, and faith itself. The presenters of secular knowledge, whether it is scientific knowledge or knowledge in the humanities, should not reject the fact that there is a larger reality known only through faith itself. However, presenting that fact and especially the way to find (be found by) and relate to God by faith is not the responsibility of these teachers. Even teaching about theology, various religions, and philosophy necessarily means teaching the beliefs found in religions and philosophies in a larger reality that surrounds the natural world, but does not require leading their students towards faith itself. However, Christian teachers know that beyond being able to describe beliefs, one's belief or faith in God itself is a gift and must arise from (be inspired in) the inner person, not simply the mind or intellect. In this sense, faith is caught rather than simply taught with words. I believe that church-related colleges should seek to have teachers like this. I believe this emphasis can be preserved better in a church-related school than in one that designates itself as Christ-centered, although I admit that this emphasis may also be present in a Christ-centered school and that a church-related school may be able to learn important lessons from a Christ-centered school.

Conclusion

The secular in education is difficult to manage because the power of the secular as methodology is not just demonstrated in science, but in all fields of knowledge. At the same time, the limitation of the secular becomes increasingly evident in higher education where students are not being challenged and also helped to make spiritual and religious decisions for life directions. Secular methodology cannot deal adequately with the meaning and purpose of life. Secondary purposes, such as career paths, can be taught with secular methodology but the same can not be said concerning the ultimate purpose that extends beyond the present life. When educational institutions, including church-related colleges and universities, become dominated by secular methodology—what Schwehn calls the Weber ethos—they become mainly job or career mills and lose the ability to teach the whole person and point students toward a vocation or a calling that is life fulfilling.[11]

Secular knowledge is available to everyone and there are established methods used by scholars in different fields for accessing and creating this knowledge which should be taught in all schools. From the Christian theological viewpoint, the secular world and secular knowledge are all related to God and Jesus Christ, through whom all things were made and exist. This affects how secular knowledge is used, but the methods of gaining secular knowledge are shared with others, whether they have faith or not. Studying and working with secular knowledge is clearly related to the faith of the Christian scholar even though those with faith and without faith can work together in gaining secular knowledge. One of the advantages of secular methodologies is that they can bring together people of all faiths and no faith in the search for knowledge. All of the above indicates that a church-related school needs to seek to be able to match the best secular or state school in gaining and teaching secular knowledge and skills.

Theological knowledge is knowledge that is believed about God, which anyone may affirm, but cannot prove in a scientific manner. Theological or religious knowledge may be false, partially true, or largely true, but even if largely true it necessarily will be partial because it is held in human minds,

---

11. Schwehn, *Exiles from Eden*, 18, 19.

which are limited. This requires humility about one's beliefs and a willingness to listen to others. In Christian churches, theological knowledge often differs among people and groups according to what is emphasized as much or more than by specific statements of belief. It is even a fact that different churches and Christian groups develop distinctive cultures by the language they use. Mainline churches and church schools, for example, are not as aggressive or as explicit in expressing their Christian faith, particularly outside of the worship setting, preferring to attract people to faith in Christ in an environment in which questions and doubts can be raised and discussed and free choices made. The danger of this approach is that it may not be explicit or clear enough about faith. The Reformed tradition to which I belong bases theological knowledge on the interpretation of God's revelation through Jesus Christ and the Bible, with the aid of the Holy Spirit given to the whole church. In this interpretation, the Bible is regarded as authoritative, but its authority is derived from Jesus Christ to whom all authority has been given. It is also very important that theological knowledge is gained, maintained, and continually improved in the community of the church so that the church itself may be reformed and continually reforming—hence the name, Reformed theology. New conditions and contexts require new interpretations of the Bible in order to improve the knowledge and service of the church to God's kingdom. In fact, the church's primary calling is to express the kingdom of Jesus Christ in its life. To that end, the church has established schools of theology who prepare "teaching elders" for the church, who are then used in both churches and schools. At present there are different traditions of interpreting the Bible that are expressed in mainline churches and evangelical churches with the result that there are different approaches to Christian education. Mainline church-related schools should not ignore the criticisms from conservative schools, but at the same time they should realize that they uphold a distinctive tradition of Christian education that always has room for improvement, and recognizes God as the author of all that is true and that all true knowledge is from God.

CHAPTER 6

Secular Methodology in the Family

THE FAMILY IS A human institution, which means *ipso facto* that it can be looked at and experienced on a secular basis. Human beings are animals, but they are more than animals because they are given the capacity to communicate with God and also to live beyond death in eternal fellowship with God. But the family is also a human institution that has a major influence in the development, or lack thereof, of a sense of the reality of God, including the sense gained through faith in Jesus Christ. The family may also transmit a secular perspective. In fact, families are a major influence in transmitting a whole host of mental perspectives that make up the cognitive aspects of individuals and cultures. Many of the perspectives may be distinct to a family and also to the community to which the parents belong. At the same time, children under the influence of others may react against the influence of their families and certainly adults often recognize how they may have changed their views from those of their childhood family, even though they may love and respect their families.

The Christian faith perspective involves an inner experience that is felt as faith and love that, if nurtured by the family and its community, will grow as a person matures. The fact is, of course, that the planting of faith and its nurturing are not easy tasks and may encounter many hindrances, whether from the family or outside the family. Christian leaders, particularly educationalists in the church, need to study the human institution of the family to understand as much as possible the dynamics of family life from both the secular sociological perspective and the religious perspective. Courses in marriage and family, or simply family, have become standard in the social sciences, and there is a lot of literature on these subjects in both the social sciences and in Christian literature.

SECULAR METHODOLOGY IN THE FAMILY

The family as a secular institution can be made (though it is not necessarily) a sacred sphere of God's special activity (a small church). At the same time, society represented by the state in modern societies has an interest in encouraging healthy and stable family life. In fact, from the beginning of human history there have been social norms and laws (the latter when writing was discovered) governing marriage relationships and care for children. The state gives permission to marry and offers protection to family members, particularly wives and children who are the most vulnerable in family situations. Sadly, social workers and the police often have to deal with domestic violence, abuse, and neglect in child care. Harmful experiences in families have always existed, but the pressures on family life causing harms to it in modern societies are especially strong. Mary Eberstadt argues that the decline of religion under modern secularization has been caused by the modern decline of the family.[1] While failed and broken family life certainly negatively affects the religious faith of its members, I believe Charles Taylor's explanation given in chapter 2 is a more basic and comprehensive theory of the secularization process. Eberhardt's conservative views, writings, and associations make her arguments suspect, but also there appears to be a confusion of correlation with causation. Furthermore, I am trying to show in this book that secularization is not an entirely negative development. Nevertheless, no one can deny that the nature of family life strongly affects faith either positively or negatively.

The idea that marriage and family life are simply private affairs is a modern false idea based on an exaggerated notion and experience of the autonomy of individuals in modern life. Marriage and families need social recognition and approval, hence marriage licenses, ceremonies, and celebrations. Families have existed as long as human beings have existed and there are even families among animals. This is because people generally are highly dependent on their families for security and support and are interested in maintaining continuity in family life. It was thought that in modern societies in which individuals have more freedom to make choices about schooling, marriage, work, and associations, that the primary relationships of the family would become less important. However, the family—especially at the nuclear level—has remained highly important for people, not only for early socialization, but for continued security and support. Family members often help adult members financially, offer shelter, help the aging, or simply provide moral support at crucial times.

1. Eberstadt, *How the West Really Lost God*.

This brief overview of family life is a reminder that just as there are secular standards for what makes daily life work well—for example hard and honest work—so there are some secular standards for what makes for a good family life in contrast to bad family life. One could say the common-sense actions leading to a good family life are secular methodologies themselves. These common-sense actions include responsibility toward and care for family members, fairness in treatment of one anther, honor for those with authority, and obedience as far as possible by family members to those with authority in the family. People of faith can learn from those without faith who may actually maintain better marriages and family life than people of faith. In addition to the secular common sense characteristics of a good family, there is much that can be learned through secular social scientific studies of marriage and family life that people of faith could and should learn. At the same time, people of faith need not discard their faith perspective in judging the value of the recommendations based on social scientific studies. These studies may leave out the influence of faith in families or they may even as secular studies demonstrate the value of faith and of mutual love. Basically, social scientific studies of the institutions of marriage and the family should be respected, examined, and participated in, the last particularly if one believes the value of faith and church life for the family may be demonstrated.

After recognizing that there are common-sense secular patterns for a good marriage and family life that may be practiced by people without faith, and that important principles for a good marriage and family life may be discovered by the secular social sciences, people of faith should recognize that they need help from God to live up to these practices and principles at every stage in life. In other words, people of faith need humility to be able to learn from all sources that which is important in the complex realities of marriage and family life. The church, of course, has an important duty to help people in their dealings with all the realities of living, which certainly include marriage and family life. A place to begin is with the need of children to have interaction with faith. In addition, all people through all the stages of life need ongoing repentance and new experiences of faith.Elderly parents need and enjoy enriching fellowship with their children, and in most cases, careful attention and care from them. For the faithful, there are numerous resources available by grace found through the Holy Spirit in prayer, the church, the Bible, and the sacraments. These can make marriage and family life into a rich and continued blessing and joy. Nevertheless, again, there are secular aspects of marriage and family life that simply belong to human beings as human beings. For example, in good child-raising or marriage practices, there is much that can be learned from simple observation, but also secular studies of marriage and the family. At the same time, there is hardly any aspect of life other than marriage and family that can benefit more by the infusion of faith at every level. This is a good example of why a secular methodology is a means to an end, but can be a good means that serves good ends. These good ends are very consistent with Christian views of marriage and family life.

Marriage

The Supreme Court ruling allowing same-sex marriage increases the level (unfortunately also the emotion and not the rationality) of debate about marriage, particularly with regard to the importance of understanding the meaning of marriage. I will state my beliefs here. Although some think (many may assume) that different genders are important in a definition of marriage, I believe a definition that has always been true of marriage and fits the present changing circumstances and understandings is: Marriage is a personal and public commitment between two people for a lifelong and physically intimate relationship with mutual caring responsibility resulting in the establishment of a family. Notice that monogamy is in this definition and I believe, besides being affirmed in the Bible, monogamy is based on long human experience in which monogamy has worked best for the large majority of people. The family may only be two people, but of course, it may be potentially larger if children are produced or adopted. Love is not mentioned in the definition, but "commitment" and "mutual caring" are certainly part of love and it is no wonder that love is the aim and ideal that has come to be accepted as a central requirement for a good marriage. Unfortunately, many people do not recognize that mutual commitment is part of married love. In addition, with committed love, an underlying element which is basic to all abiding relationships must be trust. Trust is important in all relationships, not the least of which is economic relations. In fact, trust (credit) is the foundation of a strong economy as seen in Steve Martin's comment that no one names a bank Ace Bank or Acme Bank. Fidelity Trust or First National sound much more trustworthy. Basically, trust is a necessary component of any good relationship.

Some say that what I have said about marriage above that does not mention male and female is in direct contradiction to the Bible and also the history of human beings. This is simply a difference in belief about what the Bible approves of, but also a different understanding of human history. I believe a careful study of human history and of a great number of societies, some of them quite traditional, can show that human beings have had ways of accommodating people who did not fit the majority patterns of gender distinction and sexual activity. Just as modern democracy is a relatively recent development for providing greater justice in society, so openly and officially sanctioned marriage equality is a recent human development in providing greater justice to marriages. The truth of this is not lessened by the fact that some early societies practiced a form of democracy and also had greater tolerance for gender and sexual divergence from majority practice. Some conservative Christian scholars believe that a binary pattern is written by God into creation, expressed in the male-female distinction and the ying-yang distinction, but I do not believe there is such a fixed binary pattern without exceptions. Basically, regarding the directions of the Bible, the careful work of biblical scholars, who take into account the historical context of all relevant biblical passages, has persuaded me that the Bible does not condemn homosexuality *per se,* and that my definition of marriage given above is consistent with what the Bible teaches.[2] I believe that over time the views that the majority of church scholars backed by scientific studies will prevail in society as people see the justice of them.

In past societies governed primarily by custom, families (with match makers) have had a greater part in bringing two people together so that marriage was practically a means to establishing a relationship between two families. Of course, a major goal in the past was production of children, which is not as important now. There has also been the phenomenon of plural marriage when there was either more than one wife or more than one husband (the former much more common than the latter based primarily on the wealth of the man and need of women for protection), but a witness to what is in nature regarding human relationships (only two people at a time can be united physically becoming "one body") the actual practice of most people in most societies has been monogamy by far.

My own view that is now supported by law is that the most important element in marriage is the commitment to a lifelong relationship of two people. People object that the permission for two people of the same

---

2. Rogers, *Jesus, the Bible, and Homosexuality*; Johnson, *Time to Embrace.*

sex to marry opens the door for individuals to choose to marry as many people as they might choose to love, it being obvious that people can love many people on some level. (To be provocative, people have even suggested the possibilities of marrying animals they love.) As already mentioned, what people forget is that physical intimacy, typically but not necessarily involving sexual intercourse, can only be between two people at a time. I would argue that physical intimacy between two people, especially when it involves sexual activity, is fulfilled when it is combined with a loving permanent commitment. I believe this fact makes committed love, sealed by a physical relationship, a special characteristic of a good marriage. Of course, married love cannot be reduced to isolated or single acts of physical sexual intimacy. Furthermore, it is clear that both monogamy and permanency contribute to a stable environment for children, and also contribute to the stability and continuity of the family as an institution and also contributes to the stability of the larger society.

The commitment of two people to a permanent relationship of mutual love and trust mirrors and provides a model for the relationship God desires to have with human beings. This is seen throughout the Bible as marriage is used as a means of teaching about God's faithfulness to God's people and the call for reciprocal human faithfulness to God. For example, unfaithfulness to God is seen as adultery or prostitution particularly in the Book of Hosea. In the New Testament, marriage is used as an image of the relationship of Christ to the church. The norm of one partner for life in marriage accounts for the enduring phenomenon of the recognition in societies of the "woman of the world" (or "male escort") who provides temporary sexual services to men (or women) as the nonwife (or nonhusband). Of course, as a warning against pride, even these women may have hearts of gold in literature and movies, as well as real life, compared to pious but proud and judgmental women and men. Interestingly, a harlot is part of the Davidic line.

Given human weaknesses, sometimes marriages fail. In addition, freedom from the social pressure that exists in traditional societies to maintain marriages causes divorces to become more prevalent in many modern societies. It is also true that traditional societies that do not tolerate divorces are more likely to tolerate extramarital affairs, concubines, second wives, and prostitution. It is entirely possible that same-sex marriages—although these can also end in divorce just as with heterosexual marriages—will place a new emphasis on the core meaning of marriage, which is lifelong commitment in a loving relationship. I have always found it significant that popular romantic songs explicitly recognize the permanency of true love.

Family members would like the marriages of other family members to last, especially for the sake of the children so they can have an unchanging and loving environment, the children being part of the extended family. But, of course, sometimes a divorce is the lesser evil than a home without the right environment for the children or a spouse. It is through caring love that the family transmits spiritual and material assets to the following generations. Marriage stability is also of interest to the state and society at large because marriage and family stability contributes to social stability.

Family Socialization

The family is the major institution for socializing the young to survive and hopefully thrive in life. While formal education has developed with an eye toward increasing the knowledge and skills of children and youth in preparation for adulthood, family influence has remained important. Educational institutions realize that they need the support and cooperation of families if institutions are to be most effective. As education has secularized, it has become ever clearer that families are needed for socializing the young in spiritual matters. For Christians, this is faith in God and the values and morals based on this faith as revealed in the Bible. Secularization in society has also placed major responsibility on churches for Christian nurturing, churches being extensions of families when fully vital.

The difficult issue of the relationship of the secular to education has already been discussed, but it is in socialization by the family that the inadequacy of secularism as a philosophy and lifestyle becomes apparent. Children have much to learn that is secular, such as language and ordinary social interaction skills, but I and most Christians believe everything that children learn needs to be infused with the spiritual. They need to learn that the secular exists only in the mind as a methodology for improving their thoughts and actions, including religious ones. God cannot be made a cover for incorrect thoughts or wrong activity. At the same time, the secular provides a means for believers to offer all of life to God as they carry out secular activities. In addition, parents with faith are able to give children a sense of the reality of what is beyond the secular, especially the loving and caring presence of God—something which helps give children a sense of security and peace. In other words, as this book advocates, the secular should be respected as a check on human fallibility in thought and behavior. Secular methodologies, though unable to touch on the deeper things of life, offer a variety of means of offering lives to God in service. Children seem instinctively ready to believe in God and life beyond death. They also would like to serve God if shown the way. Parents, of course, have a responsibility to provide a check on the harmful imaginations of children, without limiting their creative imaginations.

The community of faith is the larger socializing body that surrounds the family and is important for encouraging and helping families in their responsibility to teach their children the faith that underlies and supports all of life. This is an important cooperative project that involves not only weekly Sunday schools or faith development classes that extend throughout life, but also missions in the community to those in need and experiences in retreats, camps, and conferences. As important as the family is, the need for good socialization demonstrates that the family itself needs a supportive community. Children and youth need to see that there are many varieties of adults who are models for them, with a variety of spiritual gifts and expressions of faith that can contribute to the goal of serving God in all of life and throughout life.

Conclusion

The family has been a secular or natural institution throughout history and throughout the world resulting from God's creation of humanity, meaning that it belongs to the natural order. But it also belongs to the spiritual order because of the spiritual nature of human beings. It provides an important window into the nature of human beings. In other words, the family is not a religious institution *per se*, but it becomes sacred as it is offered to God. Just as nature is sacred to the person of faith, so the family is seen as sacred and faith can guide it in its formation and throughout its ongoing life over generations. However, the fact that the family belongs to the natural order means that there are important principles and norms for a happy family life that can be learned and practiced by anybody, regardless of their faith. Unfortunately, people of faith may fail in carrying out some of the important principles of a happy and stable family life, but can learn both from secular and religious studies of family life.

The social sciences and human practical living continue to reveal behaviors and social conditions that positively or negatively affect family life.

These need to be studied and considered by all people. The social sciences are an important aid in such study. However, although ideals for happy family life can be set forth and widely recognized, it is another matter to live up to them. It is at this point that faith is especially relevant for bringing healing and renewal to family life, which inevitably faces problems and failings due to human weakness and sin. As in the other aspects of life discussed in this book, grace, forgiveness, wisdom, and inspiration need to be infused into family life and these are the special gifts that come through the Holy Spirit working through the means of grace (mentioned above) with faith. No family is perfect and various negative influences are inevitable, such as hurtful behaviors and emotions. Secular common sense based on normal human morality and secular studies of principles of healthy family life can aid in family flourishing. Nevertheless, the life of faith can introduce love and mutual forgiveness, which deepen the richness of family life and make it a major contributor to a life of ever-growing faith.

CHAPTER 8

Secular Methodology in Everyday Life

To BRIEFLY REVIEW THE development so far, I am interpreting the secular as a mental construct that views life and the natural world without attributing anything to God. This may be done when there is no belief in God or in the relevancy of God, or it may be done primarily as an act of humility to protect against wrong ideas about God. The believer is still aware of God and offers secular views and activities up to God, thereby making them sacred. As a mental construct, the secular also is a label for whatever is not specifically religious. Again, believers see the nonreligious activity or organization as what can be offered to God, thus making it sacred. This presents people with the faith option to accept or not accept God's choice of us and to offer or not offer all of life to God. However, even when we believe that God is working in the world, I believe it is useful to lay aside one's personal ideas of what God is doing in order to correct or improve our ideas of what God is actually doing, and then align ourselves with God's activity. To use the secular as a methodology is an act of humility because it means listening to and learning from others. This includes others who live in and study God's world. It also means showing great respect for nature and a determination to preserve and renew it. Nature is seen as distinct from God, but an arena, just like human history, for God's activity. However, I emphasize that prior to using the secular as methodology, given human sin and the difficulties of living and understanding life, the faith perspective requires focusing on the revelation of God in the Bible and in Jesus Christ. These should be understood through the Holy Spirit in the church of Jesus Christ as expressed in the fellowship of believers. This focus prepares one to humbly learn from nature and history, particularly from other human beings.

Using the secular as a methodology is probably best known in the scientific method of study that is based, even if unconsciously, on the kind of norms described by Merton.[1] Science has developed a number of very systematic methods ranging from mathematical statistical techniques to methods of systematic observation (that may also use mathematics) that can extend back as far as the origin of the universe and the origin of human life. In addition, the humanities in secular writings in philosophy, history, literature, and the arts, can touch levels of human life that are beyond the ordinary measurements of scientific methods. Although the humanities are more likely to introduce normative or nonobjective perspectives than science, the perspective may still be a secular one. I have come to accept that all sources of secular human knowledge are complementary and offer corrections to one another so that knowledge is clarified and advanced over time. Of course, during this advancement, much faulty knowledge may be promoted before it eventually is seen as false. This may require generations.

Turning to the subject of this chapter, the secular in everyday life is a further demonstration of how the secular as methodology can be highly useful and contribute to a life of faith that is beyond and beneath the secular. According to the Bible, God gave humankind a good world to be responsible for and to take care of (Gen 1 and 2). Throughout the rest of the Bible, we learn that what is most important to God is that we live every day in God's world so as to benefit others. When we are washing dishes, cutting grass, repairing the car, waiting on tables, tending the sick, studying in school or elsewhere, or carrying out a delicate brain operation, we are doing what is a secular job that may be done with or without any thought of God. This is possible because we are using the created world that is distinct from God and given to us. The jobs are not designated as religious, and yet they are all challenges to faith because all of these tasks can be done only for oneself or they can be offered up to God and in love for others. All of these activities as well as countless others can be carried out with great effort and skill without reference to God. In that sense, they all are activities belonging to the natural world that can be learned and carried out by most people. The reality of what can be regarded as secular and studied with a secular methodology and the usefulness of this methodology is the basic reason general education has secularized.

If secular methodology is seen this way, then it can also be seen that for those who believe in God (for Christians this means the Almighty Creator, Jesus Christ, and the Holy Spirit), using secular methodology in everyday life—just as in using secular methodology in science, government,

1. Chapter 2, pp 3 and 4. Merton, 267–78, 286–324, 384–412.

education, and the family—means working for God's purposes and God's glory in all that we do. What is the secular methodology of the everyday? Just as in the approach in the various areas already discussed, there are many specific methodologies within the general methodology or approach to the secular in the everyday. One of them is hard work or diligence. My mother used to tell—me mainly because of my laziness—"Do with your might what your hands find to do," which is taken from Ecclesiastes 9:10. There are innumerable secular directions (that do not refer to God) on how to carry out daily tasks and activities from "drive carefully" to "study hard." Each task also requires certain secular skills. There are many rewards for using these skills and working hard, from satisfaction at work done well to respect and appreciation from those served or helped. Nevertheless, whatever we do well with all our might can be done for the wrong reasons and even with evil results. This is when what we do is done basically for selfish reasons.

In addition to working skillfully, with effort and honesty, there are other important elements to the secular methodology of the everyday, such as gratitude for, and even awe at, what is seen and experienced. At the same time, the conditions may call for perseverance and endurance. These aspects of the methodology of everyday life point clearly to the fact that secular methodology—whether in science, government, or anything else—may have good results, but cannot ultimately define what is good and right. For those with faith, the secular itself points to the need for faith and meaning to come from another source. From that point of view (to be discussed in the last chapter), whatever we do should be done unto God and therefore whatever we do becomes a sacred task, the goal of which is determined by God and therefore learned from God. Of course, it will always be marred by human sin, but the secular in itself by its secularity is a call for divine revelation and a response of faith.

The secular methodologies of everyday life, as in the other areas previously considered, should be able stand on their own without embellishment with religious language. This is true even though we do them for our personal faith reasons. This is a requirement of humility and of trust in the power of God to work in and through the right and good actions that we offer up to God. As we know, some who are not conscious of the sacredness of the created world may do good work and make fine contributions to life. It is also true that whatever people of faith do will have imperfections or may be mixed with false pride as when people do not recognize the source of their abilities or the contributions of others to their lives. Furthermore, all that human beings do is influenced by sociocultural forces, which means that people may do or say things well, but do or say them in support of wrong causes that are harmful to others or the world. I think of all the kind and gracious, as well as very able, people I have known who supported racial segregation, not to speak of such people who supported slavery earlier. Thus, we want to avoid too easily attributing something we do or say to God for fear of taking God's name in vain or breaking the third commandment. That is why we need the secular as a methodology not only to evaluate our everyday activities, but also to examine whether their effects are good or bad!

Jesus warned against doing acts of piety in order to be seen by others (Matt 6:1–8; 16, 17). He also said to judge those who claim to be God's servants by their fruits (Matt 7:15–20) and also not to rely on constantly referring to "the Lord" (Matt 7:21–23). Specifically referring to those who embellish their words with religious language to give them greater weight, Jesus said, "Let your word be 'Yes, Yes' or 'No, No': anything more than this comes from the evil one" (Matt 5:33–37). I believe this is a reason for much of our language to be secular.

Am I spreading secular methodologies from science, government, and education to our everyday lives? Yes, but I am also saying that all secular methodologies can and should be inspired and guided by God for those with faith. Instead of pushing God out of our lives or considering God irrelevant to our everyday lives, secular methodologies in everyday life done with faith can make God more relevant to everything we do. In this way all that we do in life becomes sacred tasks. We and society in general distinguish activities that are specifically religious from those that are not religious, but the secular methodologies of everyday life break down that distinction. In other words, cooking and working in the office are distinguished in society and perhaps in our minds from going to church, teaching a class in church, or singing in the church choir, but all tasks are made sacred by offering them to God for the good of others. The distinction between religious and nonreligious activities creates the danger of compartmentalization in which we only think of God in our activities that are specifically related to church, such as worship at church or even only in our orally or privately expressed prayers. Fortunately, many churches have lifted up service to others outside the walls of church (sometimes inside), including especially advocacy for justice, so that they are perceived as sacred tasks.

Accompanying and adding to the possible compartmentalization of religion and the secular is society's removal of openly expressed religious language and symbols from the public sphere. This came to the notice of many people, especially those who like the trappings of religion in society with the removal of prayer and Bible reading from public education, as well as at public occasions. At the same time, this requirement of religion to go underground is a call to people to deepen their faith and spiritual thought and not to depend on the outward expressions of religion in society. Legal arguments will probably continue, but the trend toward secularization in the public sphere is well established. This may be likened to the removal of the religious canopy from public life, resulting in the deepening of religious life so that it is not simply an outward expression. With the faith option, faith, gratitude, and awe can then become more genuine and pervasive in life. At the same time, a natural and humble public expression of faith can have a great effect

I contend that the recognition of the secular in everyday life can and should have a double effect of (1) strengthening the recognition of the sacredness (religiousness) and spirituality of the secular (nonreligious) everyday life by believers, and (2) increasing the emphasis on religious bodies and religious families to take up the specific and important task of religious and spiritual socialization and training. The shallowness of language appears when we realize the nonreligious can also be considered religious, and the religious viewed as secular. The secular methodology of the everyday (which encompasses innumerable specific methodologies related to everyday living and work) does draw attention to an almost inescapable fact: human beings can live in this world with no apparent problems and perhaps even apparent great success with no thought of God. (Fairly often the apparent success does not last.) The writer of Psalm 73 recognized this long ago. At first the writer is jealous of the good life of the unbeliever, but in the end realizes the personal presence of God in his life is more valuable than anything else.

The recognition of secular methodologies—for example, honest and hard work in our everyday lives—does mean that faith in God has now been made, as never before, to rely on the conscious choice of individuals. The everyday in the mentally constructed secular world means that we can choose to ignore God or the opposite—to seek and serve God in everyday life. Now, even those who are strongly influenced by religious families and have grown up in religious communities find that sooner or later they are faced with a choice whether to continue in their religious heritage and relate it to their everyday life or live secular lives as though there was nothing else. Sadly, some choose the latter, while others find that their faith is highly related to their everyday life.

Conclusion

Secularization has removed the outward religious trappings from much of life and concentrated them in the specifically religious world. This allows people to easily ignore religion or to compartmentalize it to a section, perhaps a small section, of their life. At the same time, it challenges people of faith to see more clearly the life of faith in ordinary everyday life, as well as in the tremendously important areas of education, political life, and science. The disenchantment of nature in the secularization process is a challenge to see the real sacred character of nature and of life in the everyday world in itself and especially as it is offered up to God. It is clear that the challenge to live a life of faith in the everyday world is not met by everyone. The power and effectiveness of secular methodology—particularly in science, government, and education—has caused many people to accept the "secular mind" described by Robert Coles, in which God is irrelevant.[2] The great danger in the secularization process is that the secular becomes universalized in the minds of many people so that they become followers of secularism as an ideology and God becomes irrelevant to them. This secularization of minds is aided by the historic failings of Christianity extending to the present. To those with faith, however, secular methodology offers an opportunity to live by faith, perseverance, gratitude, and awe every day.

I would like to add that my wife's recent stay in a hospital and then for two weeks in rehab gave me a new perspective on "at the name of Jesus every knee should bend in heaven and on earth and under the earth" (Phil 2:10). I am afraid that verse has fed a triumphalist attitude among Christians just like the hymn, "Jesus Shall Reign Where'er the Sun." I saw many knees bending along with backs to serve people in need, especially by certified nurse assistants (CNAs) and nurses. I thought these people were leading (through their secular jobs made sacred) in the triumphant parade led by the One who bent his knees to wash his disciple's feet. He indicated when we bow the knee (or back) in service to others we were doing it to him. What a thought for those nurses and CNAs to lighten their loads and to spread the fragrance of Christ (2 Cor 2:14)!

---

2. Coles, *Secular Mind*

CHAPTER 9

Secular Methodology in Theology

Now it is time to return to my original struggle—the relationship of secular methodology to theology and the theological method, the subject in which I was first trained after college and which is at the center of my thinking to this day. My college major was history, which has always been of great interest to me because I like dealing with facts, always interpreted of course. In fact, in my study of the reasons for variations in receptivity to religions introduced from the outside, I had to make sociology of history a special interest and read extensively on the history of various regions and their religions. Unlike in seminary where we considered how God was working in history, in college—and as I later studied the history of religions—my approach was secular. Nevertheless, I always considered or puzzled over how God is working in history, but in a cautious, yet hopeful way. Any basic or ultimate interpretation I now make of history is based on what I believe the Bible, especially Jesus Christ, revealed. Secular interpretations must be limited to human factors only, including the human side of religions (and that includes the human side of Christianity). This illustrates the back and forth between a secular methodology and theology for me.

I will simply comment here that I believe the strongest pointer (not evidence of the reality of God in the technical sense) of God working in history is the spread of the gospel of Jesus Christ in spite of all the failures of Christianity. I take this as a major encouragement to Christians (including me), but also a challenge. Based on the last words of Jesus Christ, I consider the spread of the gospel of be at the center of God's will for the world. My studies showed that a number of secular social factors were involved, but also most importantly, religious content was also important. The religious factors, as well as the secular social factors, could all be looked at from a secular perspective. I believed I was able to show that the centrality of a person—being able to relate people to the transcendent or to God—was essential to the spread of Buddhism, Christianity, and Islam, the three most wide-spreading religions. I believe this is absolutely consistent with the theological belief based on the Bible that Jesus Christ is at the center of the Christian message, and that knowledge of incarnation and contact with the divine, along with need for compassion, are basic human longings.

Christian theology has its own distinctive methodology, which according to my view, is interpreting the Bible with Jesus Christ at the center. This interpretation needs to incorporate the secular methodology of both social and natural sciences (and the work of interpretation requires the everyday secular characteristics of persistence and hard work, which, of course, need inspiration), but it is also true that theology needs to incorporate the secular methodologies used in the humanities, for example philosophy and history, but also simply common-sense observation. I have grown in appreciation for the contribution of the humanities (after my exploration in the social sciences), particularly from others who have read more widely than I have in the world of literature, including novels and biographies. Knowledge from the world of literature is not systematic and sometimes is not reliable, but often touches depths and aspects of human life that the social sciences are not able to touch. In short, theology employs a comprehensive approach that incorporates all other fields of knowledge. Interpretation of the Bible particularly includes the tools of critical analysis used for all historical and literary writings, which have increasingly used the social sciences. However, I believe a basic starting point for Christian interpreters of the Bible is the faith that God truly has interrupted history, first in choosing Israel, and then entering history in the incarnation in Jesus Christ. This faith needs to be personal in the belief that God has interrupted one's personal life and is leading it. As I have said before, with that starting point, the resurrection of Jesus Christ from the dead, sometimes considered the greatest miracle, seems very consistent with what one would expect of God interrupting history. This is certainly at the core of the proclamation of the original and the continuing witnesses, without which Christianity would not have spread around the world.

Almost all other fields of knowledge have communities of scholars who share the results of their work and submit them for critical examination (this is especially important in scientific methodology). Christian theology is ultimately the work of the Christian community which shares the basic faith that the Bible has special authority under the universal authority of Jesus Christ. In practice, because of the high level of commitment and accompanying emotion that is part of faith, this community exists in numerous subcommunities that have created various traditions of interpretation and statements of faith coming from the various subcommunities. I identify myself as belonging to the Reformed tradition of theology. However, I am glad the best of the Reformed tradition since the time of Calvin recognizes other traditions as genuinely Christian and is open to what can be learned from other Christian traditions, Jewish theological traditions, and other religions, as well as a variety of intellectual disciplines.

Theology uses the language of faith. Although theology must use language, it is dealing with the inexpressible and words can only point at what is beyond them. The reality is that God and our relationship with God is expressed as faith (or better, trust combined with love), and is supported by a community of fellow believers and pilgrims in the Way of Jesus Christ. As noted, theology is founded upon God's self-revelation, which for Christians means the Bible and above all the person of Jesus Christ. God had to accommodate this revelation to limited human thinking and language, just as Jesus Christ in his incarnation accommodated himself to being a true human with all the limitations of human beings. I don't believe, for example, Jesus was necessarily given a supernatural view of history, but one based on his personal faith.

The Bible is a story and contains many stories, as well as poetry, visions, and music, many making use of metaphorical and symbolic meanings, which all language is in some sense. In addition, the Bible is interpreted history from geopolitical to personal histories, but the Bible is more interested in the meaning of these histories than in merely reporting events. Theology is aimed at moving the heart and will, even before enlightening the mind. In reading the Bible and preparing messages from it (preachers and teachers can testify), the heart sings, as well as laments, and is moved to tears of joy and repentance together with awe. Theology is based on interpretation of the Bible with all its diverse literature, but at the same time it seeks to be rational and reasonable in order to be understood. The idea, expressed by some secular Enlightenment scholars and their modern followers, that religion or Christianity does not follow reason or is irrational is ridiculous. In fact, some Christian theologies called scholastic or orthodox are too rationalistic, leading to too much reliance on verbal expressions and literal interpretations instead of realities beyond verbal expressions.

The faith which theology seeks to express and commend to people is not based on reason, but is reasonable or makes sense. My own view is that it makes a great deal of sense that a God who created the universe would love it and want to be related to the human creatures he created. This is seen in Genesis 3, when God walks in the garden looking for Eve and Adam. (They are hiding, which is our story.) What wonderful news that God desires to be with us! The story of the Bible climaxing in Jesus Christ is exactly the kind of story expressing what I believe such a God would do to reclaim humanity and all creation for the destiny God desires for all he created.

Theology, of course, must go far beyond the limits set by secular methodology on itself to deal only with the human aspects of the revelation of God and the response to that revelation. The social sciences have had to wrestle with extreme positivism or empiricism, meaning that attention to the empirical or what can be observed and measured is certainly an emphasis of scientific secular methodology. However, I understand critical realism—now advocated by some, especially sociologists of religion—to be a healthy correction to extreme empiricism.[1] It is not surprising that the realities of human thought and life with the addition of the philosophy of critical realism should help scholars realize the inadequacies of extreme empiricism and that reality is more than the empirical.

At this point, I will simply draw attention to the fact that the social sciences examine a great deal of what theology is about: the inner life of human beings—emotions, motivations, attitudes, values, etc. These studies can be valuable for theology and general study of human behavior. What I want to stress here is that theology must incorporate the disciplines of the natural and social sciences and the valid findings and theories produced from these disciplines. But in addition, theology must include use of the secular methodologies used in the humanities and their valid findings. This is why theology has always had a close relationship to church history and also philosophy of religion. The incorporation of other fields is not simple or easy because the valid findings and theories are constantly being challenged, adjusted, and elaborated. Nevertheless, new knowledge is constantly being developed, which theology cannot ignore. This is why good theological seminaries must include scholars who are keeping up developments in various disciplines, although I believe especially that the social sciences have been underutilized in theological seminaries. Secular

---

1. Smith, *Religion*, 6–13. Smith speaks of critical realism as a "philosophy of science" (7n7).

methodologies cannot return the favor and incorporate theology and its purely nonhuman aspects. That is why I believe all who study theology should become familiar with the sociology of knowledge, which particularly examines the various influences on the forming of knowledge, including theological perspectives, as well as the effects of various theological perspectives. My basic position is that secular methodologies contribute to theology whereas theology cannot contribute to secular methodologies except as an object of study. There is a kind of one-way looking glass between the two disciplines, with theology looking at the secular, but the secular not looking at theology, except the human side of it, which is only part of theology. "Using" is a better word than "looking" because theology needs to use secular methodology for part of its work, but secular methodology cannot really use a theological perspective in its work. Thus, theology is the more comprehensive or all-encompassing discipline in its perspective, but also more dependent on subjective and normative factors. Scientific thought is self-corrective in a way that theology cannot be because of theology's basis in faith. In that sense we should be more afraid of theology's errors than the errors of scientific thought.

The above thoughts led me to believe that theology is often best known by its emphasis. For example, people who assert believing the same statements may have different emphases in their perspectives of God with one person viewing God primarily as a high judge and another as a loving and welcoming Father. Both images may be found in Scripture, but which one is the prevailing picture? Guided by Jesus Christ and his story of the prodigal son and his whole life, death, and life again, I believe the latter picture is the prevailing one. At the same time, evil which comes under the judgment of God is extremely subtle in its manifestation and mostly beyond immediate understanding, especially since evil often portrays itself as good. However, evil is basically self-destructive, often after causing much harm.

Taking the secular seriously as a mindset for use as a methodology is important because of the theological doctrines of creation and incarnation. Creation stresses the distinction, not separation, of nature from God and yet God's love of it and presence in it. The incarnation especially affirms God's love of human life by God's determination to redeem it through Jesus Christ taking on our human nature. The awesome beauty and complexity of nature also expresses God's love of creation. God has made the universe and the world as places for human beings to treasure and care for, but also places in which God is active to reclaim them and, what is most important, to reclaim them through Jesus Christ and the Holy Spirit working through human beings. Theologians and all who pursue theological knowledge (which includes more people than we realize) cannot all master a secular discipline, but there needs to be greater familiarity with the basic secular methodologies simply out of respect and love for the world God has given us, but also to help avoid the premature injection of religious ideas or simply any of our mistaken ideas about nature. The scientific approach has helped to make people more objective and cautious (humble) in their approach. We remember Merton's ethos of science includes humility.[2]

It is apparent that, sadly, religion does not necessarily bring people together with some important exceptions. We cannot help but observe that there are many Christianities. As a Protestant of the Reformed tradition, we can see that there are even major differences between those who claim this tradition as their own. In regard to American Protestantism, it is clear that at this time there are two major parties, typically known as mainline and evangelical. What has been particularly encouraging to me is that in various groups devoted to missions, particularly overseas missions, mainline (also called councilar) and evangelical leaders have had meetings and formed associations in which mission scholars from the Roman Catholic and Eastern Orthodox Churches are also active. The American Society of Missiology and the Overseas Ministries Study Center (OMSC) are examples of this type of cooperation in the United States. The social sciences have been a great aid in bringing about these cooperative efforts. I have also noticed that in various social scientific associations, people with widely varying religious or nonreligious views come together to discuss social scientific findings and theories. Thus, secular methodology can be used effectively to bring people together. Can we say that taking nature, God's creation, seriously can be a uniting force? So far, even in the political realm in which there are great differences in ideology, secular methodology has brought people together. Secular democracy brought together (and kept together so far) people of the United States under the national motto *e pluribus unam* ("out of many one") and a Constitution that is basically secular. Democracies and other secular governments have found ways of working together in the United Nations and various joint organizations and international agreements. Scientists of all nations cooperate on joint research and exploratory efforts. Secular methodology in education can bring knowledge to diverse peoples as they learn from one another with

---

2. Merton, "Normative Structure of Science," 267–75.

the single goal of developing knowledge. There are many other examples where people may gather around a secular effort. It is true that the depth of theological convictions makes it most difficult for theologians of different traditions to gather and work together, but they can find help in gathering around a common goal set by studies conducted with secular methodologies. The gathering around a common goal itself can be given a theological significance: God working through the power of his creation and also in history where various Christian inspirations (combined with Christian oppositions) have been at work (see, for example, the League of Nations and the United Nations).

Regarding a specific complaint mentioned before, one of my disappointments has been the relative lack of attention to social scientific studies of religion, particularly of missions, my area of interest, in mainline church seminaries, especially those of my own Presbyterian (USA) church. Evangelical scholars have made better use of anthropology to aid their understandings and practice of missions, particularly overseas missions. I deal briefly with this issue in the Appendix. All Christian theologies assert the importance of world history as an arena for the working out of God's will for humanity, but the interpretation of history is a complex theological task, especially the interpretation of particular events. I believe that the secular methodology of the social sciences combined with the secular approach in historical studies and reporting by experienced foreign service workers and journalists can be a great aid in interpreting history. Smith discusses in detail the ways in which humans make causal attribution to superhuman powers in the events of history and life.[3] Such often-mistaken attributions can confirm and clarify the ongoing effects of the sinfulness of human beings taught in the Bible. Beyond this, the Bible also points to the overcoming of the effects of sin in the strength of God's creation, but especially in the spread of the gospel of God's love, often in quiet and unspectacular ways by faithful people. Nevertheless, theologians need to give attention to the social sciences. I believe it would be good if courses were offered in theological seminaries in the social sciences. Some familiarity with the statistical model of study, including sampling and experimental and controlled studies, would be very useful for ministers in creating greater objectivity in viewing the world and humanity.[4]

---

3. Smith, *Religion*, 136–89.
4. See Appendix.

The major value of the social sciences is to enable theologians and church people to be self-critical or, to use the moral and theological term, humble. From a theological perspective, the church is continually in need of judgment more than the world at large. Why? Because the church has the heavy and awful responsibility of representing God and Jesus Christ to the world. This is certainly the perspective of the Hebrew prophets, such as Amos, "You only have I known of all the families of the earth: therefore I will punish you for all your iniquities" (Amos 3:2). In 1 Peter 4:17, we read, "For the time has come for judgment to begin with the house of God: if it begins with us, what will be the end for those who do not obey the gospel of God?" I might add the thought, if it has taken these 2,000 years for the church apparently to only begin to be unified and purified so that it can represent Jesus Christ to the world, how much longer will it take for Christians to clearly represent the love of Jesus Christ to the world with a unified message? Certainly, the secular method of the social sciences and other secular methods in which people set aside their religious views to be examined under secular lenses can contribute to the church's ongoing need for repentance and change. This does not necessarily mean giving up their religious views, but rather submitting them to the community of faith in which the Bible and Jesus Christ are the authorities.

Conclusion

Theology, as the most comprehensive discipline (I believe more comprehensive than even philosophy because it includes views of God), needs to make use of secular methodologies to gain understanding of God's creation, and especially of human life and history. Interpretation of the Bible, the central task of Christian theology, requires the use of secular methodologies because the Bible, though inspired by God, is also a human book. In the Bible, God accommodated himself to human language and understanding. The Bible's dual nature is analogous to the incarnation of Jesus Christ in which Christians believe that he is both divine and human.

Theology, like all human thought, is subject to error and, speaking theologically, it is subject to sin. This makes theology a particularly dangerous mode of thought because it has the task of representing God's revelation to human beings for their redemption, which is the most crucial task of the church. It is very well known that there are numerous theological traditions, some of them which are highly critical of other traditions. Secular methodologies can increase the humility of theological thought so that theologians will be more inclined to listen to theologies which are different from their own. At the same time, theology has a prophetic task to challenge all human thought and behavior. Challenging societies may be one of the best contributions of secular methodologies because they often question conventional thinking while also providing means for self-criticism. Theology can learn from this perspective. Above all, theology, which includes the doctrine of total depravity (all thought and life is affected by sin), should recognize its own frailty, partiality, and biases, understood both in its ordinary and technical meanings. Such a perspective contributes to Christian unity, which is sorely needed in today's world and increasingly will be needed in the future world so that it will believe the gospel of Jesus Christ.

CHAPTER 10

The Future of the Secular

I BELIEVE THAT THE secular as a construction of human thought and activity distinguished from religious thought and activity in the world is here to stay because it has proven to be very useful in many areas of life, beginning with science, government, and education, but extending into many other areas of life because of its ability to add to knowledge, reduce human ignorance, and produce useful results. It also reduced religious conflict, although secular revolutions (the French, Russian, and Chinese), proved to be even more destructive than religious conflict. The secular can even add to human cooperation as people meet around its ability to open up possibilities for varieties of people with various views and beliefs to contribute to common endeavors. In other words, the secular can contribute to a certain leveling and democratization of human life.

At the same time, the limits of the secular will become increasingly evident: its inability to fulfill the transcendent longings of human beings and even the danger it introduces of falling under the spell of false secular ideologies, some of which were already experienced in the eighteenth, nineteenth, and twentieth centuries. It may also create apathy toward transcendent and meaningful relationships and activities as people become overly involved and committed in some highly useful secular methodology. This is why I believe the recognition and use of the secular as a methodology can both demonstrate its usefulness by increasing knowledge, but also its limitations in the search for, and discovery of, transcendent meaning.

From a Christian theological point of view, I believe that the secular is here to stay because God desires to be freely chosen, or rather believed to have chosen us. For that to happen, theological thought and activity needs to be clearly distinguished from the secular. The old religious canopy in which religion was simply taken for granted and people merely assented to religious views and only participated in its "secondary products, features, and powers" needed to pass away.[1] In much of the past, the option to choose God has not been a clear choice because everything was religious. The paradox is that everything is religious, including secular methodology, or rather, everything becomes sacred as it is offered up in God's service. What does this mean? As a Christian, I believe God has both shown us and also empowered us through Jesus Christ and the gift of the Holy Spirit to offer up our selves "as a living sacrifice" (Rom 12:1). However, we know very well, or should know very well, that people in the past who have considered themselves Christians have certainly not offered themselves wholly to God in the pattern of Jesus Christ. We Christians have certainly not made clear to the world, except in a limited fashion, the good news of Jesus Christ and the life offered through him to all. The task to represent Christ and his gospel has been placed upon the followers of Christ, but just as God's people before Christ blurred the way to God, Christians since Christ have blurred the gospel of Christ. The major reason for the blurring of the way to God is human sin that causes people to pursue their own interests at the expense of others even while remaining religious. We can see, if we are willing, that the pursuit of selfish interests has often been through domination of others by Christians or those associated with Christians—individuals for sure, but particularly groups. The change in receptivity to the gospel after the collapse of Western colonialism has been astonishing and should be an enormous lesson for Christians.

I believe paradoxically, just as the struggle of Christians among themselves helped the secular to emerge, often in the damaging form of an ideology, the emergence of the secular is now helping to clarify what the life of faith is. This process is still in its infancy. Since we Christians have not lived the life of faith clearly enough, we must continue on the same path of following Christ to which he called us, but at the same time open ourselves to learn from people of all faiths and no faiths, also as he would have us do. Helping in this process of clarification of faith is the major contribution of the secular as methodology. In other words, the secular as methodology can contribute to saving us from ourselves and saving us for the life and task we

---

1. Smith, *Religion*, 78–80. Smith distinguishes the roots and trunk from the branches and leaves of religion, the latter representing the "secondary, derivative, and dependent" aspects of religion. He lists eighteen such aspects or "powers of religion." People may participate in the latter while avoiding the former. I believe secularization makes this less possible.

were called to fulfill: to live in the kingdom of God as God's children and to be, or at least move toward, the new humanity God wants for us.

Those who see the secular as an enemy are likely to be disappointed at the staying power of the secular and secular methodologies. Those who see the secular as supporting their secularism or secular philosophy and lifestyle may be happy for a time because they see and want the continuing option to reject belief in God and Jesus Christ, as well as any religion, or simply to consider God as irrelevant. The major difficulty they will continue to have is that the secular methodologies in themselves do not give ultimate meaning to life, which human beings seek, and consequently the secularism they construct does not have great power to draw people except as a kind of opposition to those (religious people) they deem ignorant, prejudiced, and harmful. This does not take away from the fact that the secular methodologies can contribute to moral and ethical thought, which is inherent in human thinking (i.e., professional, business, medical, and other kinds of ethics). Wise people of faith who see the secular as providing useful methodologies with which the failures of religion and religious people, especially themselves, are judged and corrected, are glad of the continuation of secular methodologies and participate in their use. However, they realistically recognize that the secular offers the temptation to resist and escape God. Religious people also recognize the even greater danger offered by the secular of compartmentalizing religion to only one part of life and thus blurring the saving power of the gospel in all of life. In other words, this last group sees both opportunity and danger offered by the secular. I count myself among the last group. I am saddened by those who absolutize the scientific method along with the autonomous individual creating a virtual religion out of the adoration of these twin gods, but at the same time I see the great value of the secular scientific method, as well as the secular methods applied to other areas of life discussed in this book. For those of us who believe in the Creator God, we see human beings from earliest times as having a choice to worship God or worship God's creation (Rom 1:25). This has not changed, but I believe the choices are being clarified and to choose secularism (the universalizing of the secular) is inherently self-punishing.

To say again, the secular in itself does not and cannot give purpose and directions for life. This is why, paradoxically, the recognition of the secular and its methodologies actually draws attention to religion—an outcome that was not recognized or anticipated by many scholars until recently. The recognition and elevation of the secular to where it stands in contrast to religion and religious methodologies or approaches is supportive of religious freedom because the purpose and directions for life are contested and need free discussion and debate that at its base is a religious and moral debate. Because the old religious canopy has been removed, there is now a new opportunity for a broader population, not just religious specialists, to take more seriously the content of religions, including both the claims made and the experiences offered by various religions. Christianity, which inescapably is a religion, should welcome the focus on religious content. This includes Christians seeking to focus on the content of their own faith and life to make sure they are representing Jesus Christ as they claim to be.

In light of the presence of the secular in civil society, especially in education, Christians must take very seriously their responsibilities in their churches and their families to convey the faith to the next generation. Churches must take more seriously their task of teaching and really nurturing both children and adults, as well as helping families in fulfilling their responsibilities to mirror the gospel. Families also need to look for help from their Christian communities. To reiterate, this emphasis on propagating the content of faith is made especially clear because government institutions, particularly public schools, must be secular in their approach. This naturally applies to all governmentally related organizations, institutions, and agencies.

Societies are united by common values. Originally, and still to a great extent, these were associated with ethnic pride and survival as a people. Nations were built upon these values and, as we have seen, religion was used to reinforce them. We can now see that Christianity became too intimately allied with nationalism. Many of the Protestant and other Christian supporters of ultranationalism in the United States and other Western countries consider themselves quite religious. This was seen before in the supporters of Franco, Hitler, and Mussolini.

Rulers and others with power may seek to impose common ethnic and nationalistic values combined with autocratic rule and may succeed for periods of time, especially if they are able to advance prosperity. They may seek to use religion to support autocracy and anti- or nondemocratic movements. We see this happening in China, Russia, and other countries. People will accept dictatorships for the price of order and prosperity, even just survival. If the civil values that unite a people are not developed in a free society, they will be imposed by the authorities. On the other hand, in societies in which democratic values have been developed, particularly through belief in human rights and lived experiences with freedom in democratic groups (often church congregations,) these democratic values become an important part of the support for a civil society in which people can be free to express what they believe, including their religious beliefs.

In the United States, a strong civil society has developed with strongly held democratic values that include upholding many freedoms—especially religious freedom—together with freedom of speech, the press, and assembly. However, if one believes in the periodic release of evil, as I believe is taught in apocalyptic thought, evil power may be supported by Americans as it was in Europe. The autocratic tendencies have already been revealed, usually with the desire to control some population group. Although the United States population was very supportive of religious freedom and religious activity, it was and is very divided religiously, ethnically, politically, and socioeconomically. Some Christian groups have sought quasi-official status, but as of yet, there has been no great support for an official religion.

I believe religions need to lead the way to a healthy civil society with what might be called a civil religion, but more accurately a civil contract based on mutually accepted ideals, which we know have a religious base, but have become secular, free-floating, and widely accepted. Regarding religions, mild or even friendly competition among religions in the United States has actually stimulated church and organized religious activities in an increasingly diverse society. Churches that are increasingly willing to listen and talk to each other have aided this process. The American government has favored religious bodies through its tax laws, as well as encouraging private education and the organization of innumerable not-for-profit organizations as important parts of a healthy civil society. Voluntarism based on a sense of obligation and responsibility for others, as well as sociability, is expected and encouraged in American civil society. Nevertheless, cultural wars have divided the nation, exacerbating the conflict between the two political parties representing different values and views or at least different emphases in values and views in American society. James Davison Hunter has written very perceptively about these subcultural conflicts in the United States.[2] I believe mainline churches have muted these conflicts, but other more dogmatic churches and religious groups have exacerbated them. At present, the mainline churches seem to be suffering from being less dogmatic. This should stimulate thorough self-examination.

---

2. Hunter, *To Change the World*.

Religious organizations are part of civil society and have every right and responsibility to make their faiths known and to advocate for just laws, policies, and programs by the government. However, I believe it is at just this point that humility demands that the secular as methodology needs to be recognized and utilized by churches. First, it is obvious that civil society contains many different religious groups with varying perspectives. Not only so, but many religions, particularly the larger ones, contain various perspectives, even subcultures. A major responsibility of religious bodies, especially Christian bodies that have been present since the founding of the nation, is to mirror how civil society and political bodies can both live in peace and bring about needed changes in a peaceful manner. One of the main contributions churches can bring to society is giving people experience in working together for a common goal. This may appear to be laughable given the many schisms resulting in numerous church bodies that have come into existence throughout Christian history, especially in recent times in America. Nevertheless, churches, organized on local, national, and international bases, and carrying out work around the world, are the major examples that diverse people can work together when they respect, accept, and love one another as fellow children of God. Skills in organizing, including parliamentary procedures, need to be learned. In spite of the large number of denominations, many Christian groups do recognize and work with one another, but much more of this is needed. We have seen this take place between Roman Catholics and Protestants more than ever before. Significantly, the use of secular methodologies, as mentioned above in the case of mission organizations, can support religions and religious people communicating and working with one another. This takes place as they meet to examine and discuss the findings of scientific studies in which normative views have been set aside.

Summary

Three approaches to the secular are likely to continue into the future. One approach has the perspective that the secular is all that there is, namely God is absent or nonexistent. This is the extreme view of those who are secularists or followers of secularism. I believe this view carries the seeds of self-destruction. In this view, religion is entirely a human creation or projection of the human mind, which is simply part of the natural world. In other words, religion, not the secular, is the mental construct. I believe this makes an idol of the secular or of the natural world, but of course religions can also be followed as idols. Many secularists are also followers of scientism or have made an idol of science. Mikael Stenmark has written clearly about scientism and its imperial pretense to provide the only reliable knowledge of reality.[3] Other secularists, particularly people in the artistic and literary fields, have made an idol of the autonomous individual. I believe the followers of secularism are primarily dangerous to themselves. However, they can be dangerous when they seek power over others, as in the case of some ideologies, as we saw clearly in the twentieth century. The major weakness of secularism is that it goes against what human beings want, namely contact with the transcendent and ultimate meaning to life. On the other hand, secularists are expressing the human religious spirit by making an idol of nature or the autonomous individual, or both.

Secondly, there is an opposite approach for some found among religious people, where they make an idol of their religion, usually selected aspects of it that they like and feel they can manage. At the same time, they regard the secular as totally evil. People who make an idol of their religion or some aspect of it often seek to impose it on others as a means of social control. The Bible (really an interpretation of it) or some authoritative figure, or both, can be used as a means of control. Historically, the secular emerged in opposition to this kind of religion. Rather than recognizing the contribution of the secular methodologies in correcting the errors of religions, such religionists react in fear that some of their ideas will prove to be false. Elevating a selected aspect of religion is equivalent to compartmentalizing religion to only a portion of life. People pay their religious dues, but then assume control over the rest of their lives that they see as their own. This is a modern form of polytheism in which various aspects of the secular take a place in devotion alongside what is considered properly religious. This view and use of the secular can also be dangerous when people make their religion conform to the often unconscious secular goals they have. Many times these secular goals are ideological and political goals that affirm religion as a good thing for society, but support particular social groups (usually with economic power) while oppressing other groups.

Finally, in the perspective of biblical faith, secular methodology deals with the sacred because God is creator of all and is continuing to work in and through all things. A secular methodology itself becomes sacred as it is offered to God in service. Moreover, the emergence of the secular has

---

3. Stenmark, *Scientism*.

revealed that religion, often contrasted to the secular, contains large elements of human thought and activity and is therefore flawed and even sometimes used for evil purposes. Thus, God has used the secular to judge and purify religion—especially Christianity—but also all nations and peoples. At the same time, much that is outside of religion and part of what is regarded as in the secular world is good because God created a good world.

From a Christian perspective, Christianity has resulted from God's self-revelation contained in the Bible and supremely in Jesus Christ. This is God interrupting and invading human history. The result has been both Judaism and Christianity. Judaism and Christianity cannot escape being religions because they are composed of humans who must organize and communicate with one another and others. Focusing on Christianity, my religion, clearly it is fallible and in need of continuing correction (judgment). Although faith is an inner capacity that is unobservable and ineffable, it is preceded and followed by many empirically observable phenomena through which God works. The major value of the secular is when it is used as a methodology to understand God's world, including both the natural *and* the religious world, at least with respect to its human side. For Christianity especially, the secular methodology of scientific study can be used to correct flawed understandings of both the created universe and the self-understanding of religions. It can be used to uncover regularities and patterns, together with irregularities and anomalies in the natural world that can then be used to benefit human beings and preserve the world. This is clearly seen in the field of medicine, but also in such mundane activities as plowing a field and planting trees and crops. Skill in medicine and farming may be learned apart from religion, although faith may and should continue to be an inspiration for Christians in all activities, especially in aiding other people and understanding and tending to God's creation.

It remains true that when a large proportion of a population profess to be Christian, others will see the actions of that population expressed in their government as representing the Christian way. This means that Christians should be among those who are willing to raise questions about government policies, especially if the dominant culture of the society is Christian. Thus, Christians and Christianity should be in some measure countercultural. This is an important reason for maintaining freedom of thought and expression in a civil society. It is also an important reason for Christians to try to influence government policies, but without religious elaboration. Justice is recognizable by human beings without religious arguments.

In the end, the secular is both friend and foe depending on how it is seen and used. It may be seen as a realm for the activity of God and used to correct and improve religious thought and life, as well as life for all human beings. The secular becomes a foe when it captures the human mind so that people turn their backs on God in all or much of their lives. The fact that now, because of the secularization process, God and the life of faith have become an option for choice (really realization of choice by God) may well be what God is working to create: a world in which God will be either openly chosen or rejected by human beings. For me this means that the most important question is not whether God exists, but what has God done and what is God doing? In other words: "Who do you say that I am" (Mark 8:29)?

APPENDIX

Secular Methodology in Missiology

THE PURPOSE OF THIS book has been to highlight for Christians and anyone else a view of using the secular as a methodology in a wide array of areas in life, beginning with science, in which a secular methodology is most obviously employed. However, the secular operation—not the foundation in which a divine origin is mentioned—of the United States government was clearly established from the beginning of the nation. I also discussed secular methodology in other areas like education, family life, and everyday life. Even theology itself needs secular methodology. When it comes to theology, my special area of interest is missiology or the study of missions. That has actually been the area in which I have written the most and where I worked out my approach to using secular methodology learned primarily in my studies in sociology of religion.

The field of missiology is intentionally interdisciplinary and has made great use of the social sciences, especially anthropology, which I believe has meant that sociology of religion and some of the other social sciences have been underused. Actually, the field of history has probably been the core nontheological discipline in the field of missiology. Over the years I was impressed that evangelical or more conservative churches made great use of anthropology, whereas my mainline church missiologist colleagues were particularly strong in historical studies of missions. I was disappointed that missiology as a field did not make much use of the formal scientific method, which especially aims to establish theories, namely explanations of mission phenomena.

I maintained membership in the American Society of Missiology and in 2012 published an article in *Missiology*, the journal of the society, entitled "Can Missiology Incorporate More of the Social Sciences?"[1] In 1986,

---

1. Montgomery, "Can Missiology Incorporate More?," 281–92.

APPENDIX: SECULAR METHODOLOGY IN MISSIOLOGY

I published an article in *Missiology* on the subject that was to be my major study interest: understanding the spread of religions in the light of insights gained from a social scientific perspective.[2] Most recently, the book *Missiological Research* has included what I consider the most thorough presentation of scientific methodology to date to be applied to the study of mission.[3] I was especially impressed by the definition of theory from a scientific perspective, along with the various steps taken in scientific research. My own feeling is that the field of missiology has not sufficiently pursued clarifying what theory is and establishing theories, particularly theories seeking to explain the great variations in receptivity to the Christian gospel.

Missiological Research, in addition to the discussion of scientific methodology, has a number of chapters by different authors related to the Assembly of God denomination dealing with the biblical and theological basis of missions, and thus establishes clearly that missiology is a theological subject. They take up the issue of integrating the secular scientific approach and theology. In this regard, I disagree on the attempt to integrate the two approaches, which I have seen earlier in the approach of conservative Christians in their use of anthropology. I believe it is better to clearly distinguish between the two approaches. In this way, the results of the secular scientific approach can be evaluated more easily by a wide range of scholars, and the theological implications drawn from the scientific evidence can be evaluated more easily by people with varying theological views. Different theological interpretations of the Bible and different emphases in thought will interpret in different ways the findings in missiological research and their implications for mission practice, but interpretation of scientific findings is an essential theological task of missiology and what makes it a theological field. I believe that to try to integrate scientific approaches and their findings with theological interpretations falsely implies that theological interpretations are scientific, when they should be considered implications or interpretations. An important value of using a secular methodology for investigation and building theories obtained by such research that I would like to emphasize however, is that people of different theological views can work together in evaluating the research even though they may see different theological implications arising out of the research. This is a major reason that the members of the American Society of Missiology, as well as other mission-oriented scholarly organizations, such as the Overseas

2. Montgomery, "Receptivity to an Outside Religion," 287–99.
3. Gilbert et al., *Missiological Research*.

Mission Study Center (OMSC) have been able to bring together people from various Christian traditions. A common faith, of course, is important, but humility in studying the secular or human side of religion makes a great contribution to Christian cooperation.

Bibliography

Achenbach, Joel. "The Age of Disbelief: The War on Science." *National Geographic* 227.3 (2015) 34–47.
Barnes, Craig. "Uncertain and faithful." *Christian Century*, 135.15 (July 18, 2018), 35.
Beck, Ulrich. *A God of One's Own: Religion's Capacity for Peace and Potential for Violence*. Translated by Rodney Livingstone. Cambridge: Polity, 2010.
Brooks, David. "The Secular Society." *New York Times*, A21, July 9, 2013.
Burgess, Walter H. *John Robinson, Pastor of the Pilgrim Fathers: A Study of His Life and Times*. London: Williams and Norgate, 1929.
Calhoun, Craig, et al., eds. *Rethinking Secularism*. New York: Oxford University Press, 2011.
Calvin, John. *Institutes of the Christian Religion*. Vols 1–2. Translated by John Allen. Philadelphia: Presbyterian Board of Publication and Sabbath-School Work, 1899.
Campbell, Colin. *Toward a Sociology of Irreligion*. New York: Herder and Herder, 1972.
Clydesdale, Tim. *The Purposeful Graduate: Why Colleges Must Talk to Students about Vocation*. Chicago: University of Chicago Press, 2015.
Coles, Robert. *The Secular Mind*. Princeton: Princeton University Press, 1999.
Durkheim, Emile. *The Elementary Forms of the Religious Life*. New York: Free Press, 1965.
Eberstadt, Mary. *How the West Really Lost God: A New Theory of Secularization*. West Conshohocken, PA: Templeton, 2013.
Ehrman Bart. *How Jesus Became God: The Exaltation of a Jewish Preacher from Galilee*. New York: HarperOne, 2014.
Froese, Paul. *The Plot to Kill God: Findings from the Soviet Experiment in Secularization*. Berkeley: University of California Press, 2008.
Gilbert, Marvin, et al., eds. *Missiological Research: Interdisciplinary Foundations, Methods, and Integration*. Pasadena, CA: William Cary Library, 2018.
"Great Ends of the Church." *The Constitution of the Presbyterian Church (USA), Part II, Book of Order*, F 1.0304. Louisville, KY: Office of the General Assembly, 2016.
Guhin, Jeffrey. "Religion as Site Rather than Religion as Category: On the Sociology of Religion's Export Problem." *Sociology of Religion*, 75.4 (2014) 579–93.
Huff, Toby E. *The Rise of Early Modern Science: Islam, China, and the West*. Cambridge: Cambridge University Press, 1993.
Hunter, James Davison. *To Change the World: The Irony, Tragedy, and Possibility of Christianity in the Late Modern Word*. New York: Oxford University Press, 2010.

Joas, Hans. *Faith as an Option: Possible Futures for Christianity.* Stanford: Stanford University Press, 2014.

Johnson, William Stacy. *A Time to Embrace: Same-Sex Relationships in Religion, Law, and Politics.* 2nd Edition. Grand Rapids: Eerdmans, 2012.

Marty, Martin. *The Modern Schism: Three Paths to the Secular.* New York: Harper & Row, 1969.

Merton, Robert K. "The Normative Structure of Science." In *The Sociology of Science*, edited by Norman W. Storer, 267–75. Chicago: University of Chicago Press, 1974.

———. "Science, Technology and Society in Seventeenth Century England," *Osiris* 4.2 (1938) 360–632.

Montgomery, Robert L. "Bias in Interpreting Social Facts: Is it a Sin?" *Journal for the Scientific Study of Religion*, 23.3 (1984) 278–91.

———. "Can Missiology Incorporate More of the Social Sciences?" *Missiology* 40.3 (2012) 281–92.

———. "Receptivity to an Outside Religion: Light from Interaction between Sociology and Missiology. *Missiology* 14.3 (1986) 287–99.

———. *Why Religions Spread: The Expansion of Buddhism, Christianity, and Islam with Implications for Missions.* 2nd edition. Asheville, NC: Cross Lines, 2012.

Rogers, Jack. *Jesus, the Bible, and Homosexuality: Explode the Myths, Heal the Church.* Louisville: Westminster John Knox, 2009.

Schwehn, Mark R. *Exiles from Eden: Religion and the Academic Vocation in America.* New York: Oxford University Press, 1993.

Smith, Christian. *The Bible Made Impossible: Why Biblicism is Not a Truly Evangelical Regarding of Scripture.* Grand Rapids: Brazos, 2012.

———. *How to Go from Being a Good Evangelical to a Committed Catholic in Ninety-Five Difficult Steps.* Eugene, OR: Cascade, 2011.

———. *Moral, Believing Animals: Human Personhood and Culture.* New York: Oxford University Press, 2003.

———. *Religion: What it is, How it Works, and Why it Matters.* Princeton: Princeton University Press, 2017.

———. *The Sacred Project of American Sociology.* New York: Oxford University Press, 2014.

———. *What is a Person? Rethinking Humanity, Social Life, and the Moral Good from the Person Up.* Chicago: University of Chicago Press, 2010.

Smith, Christian, ed. *The Secular Revolution: Power Interests, and Conflict in the Secularization of American Life.* Berkeley: University of California Press, 2003.

Smith, Christian, and Melinda Lundquist Denton. *Soul Searching: The Religious and Spiritual Lives of American Teenagers.* New York: Oxford University Press, 2005.

Smith, Christian, and Patricia Snell. *Souls in Transition: The Religious and Spiritual Lives of Emerging Adults.* New York: Oxford University Press, 2009.

Smith, Christian, et al. *Lost in Transition: The Dark Side of Emerging Adulthood.* New York: Oxford University Press, 2011.

Spencer, Herbert. *The Study of Sociology.* Ann Arbor, MI: University of Michigan Press, 1961.

Stark, Rodney. *For the Glory of God: How Monotheism Led to Reformations, Science, Witch-Hunts, and the End of Slavery.* Princeton: Princeton University Press, 2003.

———. *One True God: Historical Consequences of Monotheism.* Princeton: Princeton University Press, 2001.

BIBLIOGRAPHY

———. *The Rise of Christianity: How the Obscure, Marginal Jesus Movement became the Dominant Religious Force in the Western World in a Few Centuries*. San Francisco: HarperCollins, 1997.

Stenmark, Mikael. *Scientism: Science, Ethics, and Religion*. Burlington, VT: Ashgate, 2001.

Taylor, Charles. *A Secular Age*. Cambridge, MA: Harvard University Press, 2007.

———. "Western Secularity." In *Rethinking Secularism*, edited by Craig Calhoun et al., 31–53. New York: Oxford University Press, 2011.

Weber, Max. *The Protestant Ethic and the Spirit of Capitalism*. Translated by Talcott Parsons. New York: Charles Scribner's Sons, 1958.

———. "Science as a Vocation." In *From Max Weber: Essays in Sociology*, translated and edited by H. H. Gerth and C. Wright Mills, 129–56. New York: Oxford University Press, 1967.

"Westminster Confession of Faith, Shorter Catechism, Question 1." 7.001. *The Constitution of the Presbyterian Church, Part I, Book of Confessions*. Louisville, KY: Office of the General Assembly, 2016.

Wuthnow, Robert. *Boundless Faith: The Global Outreach of American Churches*. Berkeley: University of California Press, 2009.

Index

Argall, Gerald L. (Jerry), xxii

Barnes, Craig, xxii
Beck, Ulrich, 36
Bennett, Robert (Bob) xxii
bias
　as technical term, 5
　in social sciences, 6
　universality of, 5
breaking the third commandment, xii
Brooks, David, xi

Calhoun, Craig, 22n12
Calvin, John, xx, xxii, 1, 2, 95
Campbell, Colin, 19
Christianity
　as a religion, 110
　based on widespread belief in
　　resurrection, 44
　belief in interruption of history by
　　God basic to, 44
　special responsibility of when in a
　　majority of population, 110
church
　authoritarianism of, 30, 31
　clarification of nature of authority
　　of, 33
　fall of, 30
　humiliation of, 34
　institutionalization of, 30, 31
　opposition movements to, 32
Clydesdale, Tim, 69
Cogswell, James A., xxii

Coles, Robert, xvn5, 18, 36, 92
critical realism, 42, 43, 45, 96, 97

Duncan, George, xxii
Durkheim, Emile, 3, 3n6, 6n14, 46

Ehrman, Bart, 15n3, 44
Earnhardt, Eugene I. (Gene) Earnhardt,
　xxii
Earnhardt, James (Jim) Earnhardt, xxii
Eberstadt, Mary, 79
everyday life
　not needing embellishment with
　　religious language in, 89, 90
　spreading fragrance of Christ in, 92,
　　93

faith
　compartmentalization of, 30
　personal, not private, 22
　priority over feelings of certainty, xiii
faith option, x, xi, xviii, 9, 13, 16, 17, 19,
　20, 29, 87, 88, 90, 91, 92, 102, 103
family
　as human institution to be
　　understood, 78, 81, 85
　need for support from community of
　　faith of, 85
　remaining importance in modern
　　societies of, 84, 85
　state interest in, 79, 84
　strong effect on faith, 79, 86

INDEX

Federation of Protestant Welfare
  Agencies, lessons from experience
  in, 74
Froese, Paul, 16n4, 35n5

Gilbert, Marvin, 11n3, 112n3
government
  exceptionalism of U.S. based on
    broken alliance between one
    religion and one ethnicity by, 51
  moral issues very important in, 54, 55
  non-Christians may have higher
    morality than Christians in, 55
  religious foundation of U.S., but
    secular operation of, 51
  religious rationalization not allowed
    in legislation in, 59
  unlike science in need for an ideology
    of, 51
  vibrant civil society created by
    disestablishment of religion by, 57
Graham, Hugh Richard (Dick), xxii
Great Ends of the Church, 61, 68
Greenawalt, Bruce, xxii
Guhin, Jeffrey, 13

Huff, Toby E., 36n2, 39
Hunter, James Davison, 106

ideas of God, construction of, xiv, xvi,
  xvii
Industrial Revolution
  creation of great wealth by, 58
  injustices of stimulated rejection of
    Christianity, 34, 58
  increased sense of autonomy, 21
  made possible by scientific
    movement, 26
  power of church replaced by power of
    businesses by, 58
  raised standard of living for some,
    but brought suffering to many
    others, 34
  reaction of injustices in, 29

Janes, William (Bill), xxii
Joas, Hans, xn3, xin3, 36n6

Johnson, William Stacy, 81n2

Kao, Chun-Ming, xxii

Legerton, Fitzhugh, xxii
Lily Foundation funded study, 68, 69

Machiavelli, 41
marriage
  belief about same-sex, 81
  committed love and trust basic in, 81
  definition of, 81
  model for relationship to God of, 83
  monogamy dominant practice by far
    in, 82, 83
  permanency in popular romantic
    songs about true love in, 84
marriage made in hell, 31
Marty, Martin, 17
Merton, Robert K., 3, 4, 5, 38n2, 51,
  88n1, 90, 98
missiology
  need for clear distinction between
    theological and secular
    approaches in, 114
  need for social sciences in, 113
Montgomery, Robert L., 1n1, 5n11, 39n4,
  47n9, 111n1, 112n2

Overseas Ministries Study Center
  (OMSC), 114, 115

panentheism, xi
priority of faith over feelings, xiii
Protestant Reformation
  challenge to church by, 16, 32, 52, 64
  deligitimized distinction between
    fully committed and less
    committed believers, 28
  geopolitical movements in, 33
  made secularization possible, xi, 16
  radical devaluation of outer ritual in
    favor of inner life of faith, 28
  return of scholasticism after the, 28
  supported by nationalistic
    movements, 14, 16, 32

INDEX

religion
  mutual attraction to power of, 31
religious canopy, x, xvi, 11, 13, 16, 17, 19, 20, 29, 91, 102
  Assent to "secondary products, features, and powers" in, 103
Riddle, Robert E. (Bob), xxii
rights of individuals, based on Divine creation, 21
Robinson, Charles, xxii
Robinson, John, xxii, xxiin7, 10
Rogers, Jack, 82n2

Schwehn, Mark R., 62, 63n5, 66, 71, 76
science
  based on realization of God as God of order, 26
  Christianity essential to inauguration of modern movement of, 38, 39
  critical realism in, 42, 43
  institutionalization of, 15, 26, 27, 38
  motivation important in choice of topic to study in, 45
  norms and ethos of, 3–7, 38, 40, 51, 62, 98
  one-way looking glass between theology and, 45
  opposition of some Christians to, 35, 47, 48
scientism, 14, 36, 108
secular
  as friend or foe, 111
  as helping to clarify faith, xi, 104, 105
  as label, xiv, 23
  as not opposed to faith, xvi
  definition of, xi
  here to stay, 103
  inability to find ultimate purpose and meaning by, 48
  in form of two mental constructions, xi
  made sacred, 23
  three reactions to, 108–110
  unifying possibilities by, 99, 103
secularization
  as a number of processes, xv
  banner carried by Marxism, 16

  clarifying faith, xi
  created distinct realms of religion and secular, 12
  combined with emergence of autonomous individual, 21
  different routes of, 17
  disputed meaning of, 35
  dual effects of, 16
  effect on various fields, 20
  failure of, 16, 17
  made possible by Protestant Reformation, xi, 16
  opposite effects in two tracks of, 18, 19, 20
  not requiring discarding of faith by, 36
  supported by both religious and anti-religious people, 9, 15
  taking place worldwide, 14
social sciences
  additional and complementary knowledge gained in humanities to, 50 community of scholars in, 50
  considered by some as soft sciences of not real science, 41
  difficulty of studying inner life in, 47, 48
  followed development of natural sciences, 41
  lack of mainline church seminaries participation in, 49
  religion a causative factor in, 47
  sociology of religion somewhat marginal in, 46
Smith, Adam, 41
Smith, Christian, xn2, xvn6, 2n5, 6, 7, 8, 13, 20n9, 21, 36, 40, 42, 43n7 65n7 96n1, 99n3, 103n1
Smith, W. Michael, xxii
Smith, Robert M., xxii
Spellman, William (Bill), xxii
Spencer, Herbert, 5, 13
Stark, Rodney, 3, 5, 38, 47
Stenmark, Mikael, 108

Taylor, Charles, xin3, 22, 25, 28, 79

territorial concept of kingdom of God
  rejection of, 31
  supported by apocalyptic thought, 31
theology
  comprehensiveness of, 101
  inadequacy of words in, 96
  interruption of God in human history
    basic belief in, 95
  distinct from secular approach in, 94
  emphasis important in, 98
  method of, 95, 96
  more dangerous than science, 98
  need for self-criticism through social sciences in, 101
  not based on rationality, but makes sense, 97
  spread of gospel in history best pointer to God's work in history, 94
  two parties in Protestantism in, 99
  usefulness of social sciences in, 97, 100
  work of Christian community of, 95

Weber Max, 3, 46, 62, 66, 69, 76
Weber ethos, 62, 63, 66, 69, 76
Wuthnow, Robert, 22n11

www.ingramcontent.com/pod-product-compliance
Lightning Source LLC
Chambersburg PA
CBHW072154160426
43197CB00012B/2375